Other People's Treasures:

Selling on Amazon.com

Anthony Ravenscroft

Fenris Brothers
an imprint of the Crossquarter Publishing Group
PO Box 8756
Santa Fe, NM 87504-8756

Other People's Treasures

ISBN: 1-890109-54-1

Printed in the USA

Library of Congress Cataloging-in-Publication Data

Ravenscroft, Anthony, 1958-
Other people's treasures : selling on Amazon.com / Anthony Ravenscroft.
p. cm.
ISBN 1-890109-54-1 (pbk.)
1. Amazon.com (Firm) 2. Electronic commerce. 3. Internet bookstores. I.= Title.
HF5548.32.R38 2005
381'.45002'02854678—dc22

2004028532

Thanks

Primarily, those responsible for this book are long-ago dead. I'm referring to the people who figured out how to tell stories (fictional and otherwise), how to write them down, how to assemble a book, and how to get books into the hands of appreciative readers.

I appreciate the unwitting aid of the coffee shops that have allowed me to sit for hours, pounding away at my old PowerBook. This project was greatly aided in Santa Fe by Las Chivas (I hate flavored coffee, but these people make a white mocha that could too easily become my major food source) and in Minneapolis by my camping out at The Magpie (Cedar and 42nd) with occasional side-jaunts to The Anodyne (Nicollet and 44th) and the Hard Times (West Bank), the latter of which is possibly the only place on Earth where you can order a full vegan meal while smoking. Magpie and Anodyne also have wi-fi, so you've really got to stop in if you're near.

My mother, Sherry Blokzyl, taught me to be fascinated with the potential of the written word. Thanks, Mom, for the ability (and the drive) to understand this world.

Writing this was, in a small but important way, for the young people in my life, to show them what I do with my unexciting life. So, to my various nieces and nephew, and most especially my kids Graeme and Inanna: If you can imagine it, you can do it.

Contents

Making the Amazon voyage

Let me start by being honest: you probably won't get rich by selling stuff on the Internet.

First of all, the odds are against you, for many reasons. There are thousands of people out there already doing the same thing, so they have established experience and connections. Many of those people have areas of special knowledge, and there's no way that you can leap in and begin competing with that. Some of those folks are representing or working for companies that have assets you probably can't match, or a merchandise selection you can only dream about. At the very least, they've already got the track record, the reputation.

Secondly, selling on the Internet looks easier than it is. Sure, there's a thousand sites that give you the *opportunity*, and almost as many little companies that are more than happy to sell (or lease) their software packages and technical support and sales kits and space on their sites. Fact is, though, this all boils down to giving you a table at a flea market or your own corner at their garage sale. There are many places that give you the opportunity, but few that have the Internet "foot traffic" to give you a reasonable chance of selling your items at a good price. Most of these sites are only visited by a few thousand unique individuals every year.

At that point, the pressure is all on you. You have to go out and market your selection, somehow make the world aware that you have something to offer, then convince them to show up and sift through your listings. This marketing will probably take up more time and effort than everything else added together. In the end, you wind up with less advantage than the "generous" provider of the site, since it is they who benefit from the cumulative traffic driven to their site by you and a hundred others like you.

Altogether, you could end up with a couple of boxes of merchandise that nobody wants, competing head-to-head with folks offering much cooler stuff at prices lower than what you paid for your own stock.

You may have thought about this already, and decided that it's just not worth the time and the worry only to look forward to many hours of hunting for where the semi-mythical potentially interested people congregate, then convincing them to shop and – hopefully! – buy.

Let's dream a little. Say that there was a way that makes it easy to put your list of merchandise on display, a way that doesn't cost you much as far as time or money or effort, a way that draws potential customers and makes it easy for them to browse and choose and buy. While we're dreaming, let's hope for an easy way of processing orders and collecting payment.

What I'm proposing is to show you how to take stuff that costs you next to nothing – or less! – and put it out for purchase at a pretty good flea market that charges you nothing up front. Yes: nada, zip, zero. And when you *do* sell stuff, they take only a modest bite.

That flea market is known as **Amazon.com**. It is the ultimate world-wide garage sale, open 24 hours a day, seven days a week, 365.25 days per year, viewable by anyone on Earth (and probably a few other planets) with access to a Web browser. Thousands of people visit that site every *hour* – possibly looking for the very item that you happen to have.

Confessions of a bibliomaniac

My company started selling merchandise on Amazon.com in 2002 for a variety of reasons. I'm going to have to play coy at that point and not tell you what that company is, what our main "real world" trade is, or even give the name we go by on Amazon.com – not because I happen to like withholding information from exemplary people such as yourself but because it might be bad for business.

What I *can* tell you is that I'm a book nut. I read voraciously (about a book a week, no matter how busy my life happens to be), I've studied the history of printing, and I know enough about bookbinding and papermaking that I can reduce most people to glassy-eyed staring in a matter of minutes – one "friend" (you know who you are) suggested I hire myself out to extract confessions from hardened criminals, probably by describing the evolution of the sewn binding. In short, I'm a fanatic.

It's not an exaggeration when I say that there are used-book sellers and thrift-shop managers who know they've made their quota for the day when I walk in the door. I can't help myself. There are the many books that I want, and the books that I know my friends will want, and then there are the books that I'm not interested in personally but are simply too good a deal to pass up.

Over the years I'm certain that my assorted roommates and spouses have considered getting together to perform an intervention. You know: "Tony, we all love you, and we're worried about this behavior," that sort of thing. But then they start looking over the titles overflowing the shelves and packed into boxes and stacked in the corners, and within minutes they're lost in some fascinating obscure book that grabs their attention and takes hold of their mind.

That was when I began to figure out that maybe my lot in life is to be a purveyor of really neat books, and finding proper homes for them. I have the gifted eye to spot the merchandise… but I was a bit lacking at finding the demand.

For a couple of glorious years, I had my own little bookstore, Raven's Wing. Normally, a bookseller deals with wholesalers and distributors, digs through the lists and catalogues, then writes a sizable check for dozens or hundreds or even thousands of books and related items (calendars, bookmarks, backpacks, that sort of thing). Unless you want to sell just the same old stuff as every other dealer, you'd have to go through multiple suppliers, sometimes highly specialized themselves, and more than a few small publishers who didn't have a distribution deal with any of the big players. Then your money sits on the shelf, yellowing and gathering dust, until someone walks in the door and offers to turn that merchandise back into cash, maybe even with a little profit.

I enjoyed that, but I couldn't help feeling that there ought to be more to it. The process seemed so sterile, so mechanical, so obvious. In order to even spark a notice against the big chains, my store would have to have a thousand titles. Each day that a book sits on the shelf is a day closer to closing the shop – when you're renting a space, you're paying for every day, every hour, every minute, even if the lights are off.

We gave ourselves a little bit of an edge by playing to the neighborhood we were in. Bless their hearts, we got ourselves adopted by our neighbors, who would stop in with us first when looking for gifts, and maybe chat for a few minutes over a cup of tea.

We further improved on the edge by focusing on books that dealt with New Age topics, alternative healing methods, Eastern philosophy. Again, rather than having to browse through an acre-spanning store crammed with shelves, someone interested in those topics would check with us first. I wasn't sure this was a winning strategy, until we had a customer, on her second visit, drop a huge stack of books on the counter (at the time, I was certain that it comprised about five percent of our total inventory) and calmly write out a check for $250. A week later, two tourists from Nova Scotia, on their way to breakfast, were so enchanted with us that they each spent $100. We offered a conveniently concentrated selection, and many times brought in related books that, in a bigger store, might be separated by a hundred yards if they're available at all.

I was lucky enough to have a local wholesaler as part of my supply network. A retailer such as me was free to visit their warehouse with three stories of shelved merchandise, and simply fill up one shopping cart after another, send these carts downstairs with an identifying note, then enjoy a cup of coffee while the whole mess was totted up and packed into boxes.

On one of my first visits, I strolled around a corner and bumped into a somewhat chaotic area. This was where they stacked the remainders, the cutouts, the odd lots that they'd acquired elsewhere, or maybe found in an old box in their own dark corners. There were a few small out-of-print hardcovers about the lore of various herbs. At 25¢ each, I scooped up a handful, figuring that my customers would enjoy them as curiosities.

The advantage of managing your own shop is that there's really nothing confining you as far as price – it's largely a matter of what the traffic will bear. Out of curiosity as to what that was, I took these little books and put them out at half their $14.95

marked retail price, figuring I could always shave this down until they sold, since I'd paid such a pittance.

Within two weeks I'd sold them all at $7.50 each.

I felt a little guilty at first. Then I rationalized it: each customer got a new, unmarked book, a title they were unlikely to find elsewhere, for half what they would have paid at the big stores. And, besides, I now had a few more dollars to pay toward the rent, to get more merchandise, and to otherwise continue providing our customers with a trickle of neat stuff.

The next month, I went to a housewarming for two friends who'd fallen in love, gotten engaged, and together found a house. As part of the process, they were clearing out their respective accumulations of stuff, and after various garage sales and giveaways were down to the remnants they simply wanted to have gone. I took a dozen books, including a very nice oversize hardcover about tigers, and my friends refused to accept a cent.

The tiger book sold a few days later for $25.

I knew that I was onto something, but I couldn't figure out what. After all, if I had unlimited funds, I could think of a worse fate than sitting in a dingy shop crammed with thousands of mouldering tomes, buying up box after box of additions from people clearing out Aunt Martha's attic, and maybe even selling the occasional beat-up treasure for a few dollars' profit. The sticking point was that "unlimited funds" part: I'd need to not only pay the rent on said shop, and buy those boxes for a pittance (not zero), but handle little things like paying for a place to live, food, and the occasional extravagance like car repairs.

When landlord problems forced us to shut our doors in 1992, I oversaw a couple of big sales where we disposed of almost all the inventory at cost. We were never able to reopen, but I knew I was on the verge of something new.

Then, technology happened

Al Gore never actually claimed to have launched the Internet. Still, with all those people who want to besmirch him for making such a claim, I figure he deserves some balancing kudos. Therefore, bless you, Al Gore, for this dubious, fascinating miracle, or at least for your role in making it a public service.

To trim an already long story, I discovered the mixed joys of on-line shopping, and I was hooked. In 2000, I was grabbing books from Amazon.com that I'd wanted for years, and usually getting them at a low price; despite a few glitches with the mechanics of payment, my ratings as a buyer on eBay steadily rose. I tried a few other auction and sales sites, and still have active accounts in a handful, but those two generally satisfy my obsessions: books, music, and aging technology (this book is being written on a circa-1990 Apple PowerBook purchased from a credible eBay seller, along with a bunch of accessories, for less than $75).

Still, the Siren's song of those real-world bookshops lured me. When a thrift store is selling old novels for a dime each, my common sense goes out the window. Ditto when the big chains are clearing out remaindered copies of titles I'd wanted to read for only three or four dollars each, with a torn dustjacket slashing the price to a dollar or even less. Despite the Internet allowing me to target my purchases with deadly precision, I was still accumulating good books at a prodigious rate.

When my employer expressed interest in using eBay to unload some excess items, I looked into it. The maze of options daunted me. In order for a merchant to make optimum use of eBay, there are scads of picture-hosting services, hit counters, and payment methods. Then I would have to figure out how to present each unique item and carve out a page, and worry about setting opening prices and minimums. After all that was settled, I had to think about what to do about ensuring payment, as a surprising number of eBay "winners" disappear before the purchase is complete.

Okay, I'm lazy. I felt that there had to be a better way to do things, some way that didn't demand so much work, that left out most of the suspense of an auction, and that protected me from buyers who wouldn't pay.

And that brings us up to the part of the story where you come in.

What this book will give you

There are plenty of item categories you can sell on Amazon.com. You can move items under their groupings of Tools & Hardware, Camera & Photo, Computers, Outdoor Living, Kitchen &

Housewares, or (thankfully) Everything Else.

I'm preaching *focus*, though. Most of those categories cannot be sold outside of the United States, for reasons varying from sheer hassle factor (it's a pain to ship a used refrigerator to Indonesia) and oddnesses of copyright law, to international trade agreements or even national security.

My company sells small stuff – easy to acquire, store, pack, and ship. Computer games and other software can't be freely traded across borders via Amazon.com, so we've skipped that for the moment. If we ever want to diversify, or we hire someone who's more knowledgeable about those areas than the present staff, that might change.

For us – and, I suspect, for you – the best trade is in DVDs, videotapes, music CDs, and books.

Bookselling is, in this Internet age, a seeming anachronism. What with all the technology clogging up our lives, the flinging of physical books back and forth around the world hardly seems like a big winner. Books, after all, are pretty much what they've been for centuries: wads of printed paper stuck together at one edge.

But computers and electronic communication have proved to be a huge boon for the trade. Books are everywhere, and sometimes can be carted out of peoples' homes to effusive praise and heartfelt thanks. Millions of the darned things are poured into our lives every year. As one critic has pointed out, nobody knows why they sell in the first place, who is buying them, or how to best put the product before its ideal market. The result is that thousands of copies seem to end up in a pile in some dank corner of the world while the very people who'd gladly buy them at sometimes overinflated prices don't even know the title was ever published.

All we needed was a way to inform those potential buyers. Now, we've got that... or the necessary technology, at least.

A decade ago, up popped a company that decided to make a difference, and to make a profit from it. They invested many millions of dollars in hardware, in custom software, in advertising and in marketing. They knew it'd be years before they made back their investment, but the cash would roll in steadily once that great day was reached, if they only laid down a solid foundation.

That's Amazon.com. And, sensing that there was money to be made, they left the door open for the small entrepreneur, like you and me, to join them.

There are a few ins and outs, of course. Every art and craft and occupation has its own techniques. Something that might seem simple (like, say, selling books on the Internet) has a set of basic skills, rounded out by "tricks of the trade" that make things easier and add to profit potential. For the trade in which I participate, a successful enterprise needs to know a little about books, a little about the Internet, a little about basic business operations, and a little about how Amazon.com works.

Well, I know about as little as anyone else. If I can make a go of it, chances are that you can too.

The reality

I have a maxim for you, and I want you to remember it often:

> **When you sell on Amazon.com, you are competing with people who each claim to have thousands of items listed, possibly more than 50,000 items. Many of these sellers have absolutely no idea of how to achieve a reasonable rate of return, how to value the time they spend on the pursuit of sales, or even how to tell whether they are simply making a profit.**

If you pay attention to what I tell you, you will be able to do those three things. Thus prepared, you will not be competing with them at all – you will be succeeding.

Last confession: why I'm doing this

A few months ago, someone asked me what I was going to do with my weekend. I said, "Gonna start writing a book about how to sell stuff on Amazon." His reactions were predictable:

He laughed at the idea of me writing a book. Well, that's fair.

Then, he laughed at me for being dumb enough to not only encourage competition, but to give away my company's secrets. Now, *that* I have to take issue with.

If you and me have real-world bookstores next to each other that specialize in something like new mystery novels, then we either have to spend every day cutting each other's throats to pay the rent, or carefully agree as to how we're going to split the territory. On the other hand, if we both sell used books at a decent price, not only do we offer customers the selection of one bigger store, but each of us probably gets our inventory from entirely different sources: I spend a few hours a week at estate sales, you pick up what's left from your church's frequent tag sales. Then, there's the matter of what each of us, as ornery individuals, knows and enjoys. You know a lot about romances and I'm a science fiction fan; I'm not interested in thrillers, you don't get into British mysteries. Sometimes, I bring a case of books over to you that aren't in a genre I know well, and you do the same. In short, we combine our strengths in a way that would be difficult for one bigger store.

That's how it works on Amazon.com. If you and I each have 5,000 books for sale, I'll bet that we have no more than ten titles in common. While on the surface we're competing for the same customer with $10 to spend, this is overpowered by the fact that together we're offering a bigger selection that will attract more customers overall. Everybody wins: you, me, Amazon, and the ever-important customer.

I'm happy to share these tips with you, because if you pay attention to what follows and also manage to earn a profit, it only makes for a better marketplace.

Welcome!

Moving into the Amazon community

Amazon.com: the store for dummies like me

I'll admit, I buy on eBay. Compared to the options presented by eBay, whether to a buyer or to a seller, Amazon.com is, well, kinda dumb. You walk in, choose what you want, agree to pay, and wait for your merchandise to arrive. If you want to buy from an individual seller rather than new from the company itself, you browse over to the "back pages" behind the main product description and have a look at what's listed. There's not a whole lot of excitement in the purchase process on Amazon.

One fateful day, having put selling on the eBay option behind me, I was browsing Amazon.com yet again, and I decided to click a little tag marked **Sell Items**.

I was enchanted at the lack of flexibility. There were few decisions to confuse me. Within a week, I was in charge of a simple **Amazon Marketplace** account that began to clear out not only some of my company's accumulation but my own excess of treasures.

At this moment, writing this manual, we manage almost 1,000 Marketplace items, selling a dozen per month, usually at a gross profit margin of somewhere above 75%, or a markup between 65% and – hold onto your hat – 99%. In ugly cash numbers, this operation brings in a monthly $50 to $300 gross profit. Not enough to retire on, but a pleasant income for enjoyable work we can do almost anytime, two or three hours a week.

You can do this. Sure, it takes intelligence, knowledge, skill, and diligence to maximize your profit, but if you have the drive to acquire these abilities, I will show you how.

Basic mechanics

There are a few different ways that merchandise moves through the Amazon.com site (and by "people" I mean individuals, bookshops, CD stores, publishers, and home-based businesses alike):

- Amazon.com orders from the publisher
- people open a zShop "storefront"
- people sell at auction
- people sell through the Marketplace

Unless you're a publisher, there's nothing you need to know about the first (and it's a topic for another book anyway). Later, I'll touch briefly on the second and third methods. Most of this book, though, is about that last one, which I have found to be surprisingly powerful – and profitable.

When you list a book or CD or video as a Marketplace item, there's really not much for you to do.

- Almost all sales are made only with Amazon Payments – no credit cards, no "the check is in the mail" problems or "my dog ate the money order." If the customer doesn't have an account in good standing, they can't buy, period. If their account is sound, then payment goes through, usually within minutes.
- Amazon decides how much of a cut they take from a completed sale – and tells you how much this will be when you list the item, then remind you when it sells.
- Amazon decides how much you're going to get for shipping costs. Again, they tell you at the time of listing.
- You have only 200 characters to describe your item – no photographs, no HTML, no hyperlinks, not even any bold or italic, just straight text.

When you make a sale, Amazon credits your merchant account, which is electronically transferred every two weeks to your bank. (If you make a request, they can put this transfer through more often, usually within 24 hours. Some of us prefer the regularity, though, and to date I've only had one transfer come through a little late due to computer problems at Amazon.)

At first blush, this may seem high-handed, especially if you're already experienced with eBay or some other sales or auction sites where profitable chaos is the name of the game.

Another way to look at Amazon's brusque style, though, is as a streamlined marketing method. If you need a computerized accounting system, a simple cash register is hardly going to suit you… but if all you need is the cash register, or just a metal box for change and receipts, why mess around with a computer system? Likewise, if you don't need something as all-out flexible and powerful as eBay, why mess around?

Getting started: what you need

As far as overhead or equipment or fees, selling on Amazon has to be one of the cheapest routes imaginable in the history of the human race and its business ventures.

- You need to have access to the Internet, at least every few days. As far as I can tell, you could run an Amazon Marketplace business from the public library. However, Amazon does insert a few harmless cookies to track your movement and interests, so your whole operation will go a little better if you use a private computer, the same one for most of your Amazon transactions.
- You need inventory. (Don't laugh.)
- You need a checking account at a bank or credit union in the United States. We'll look into that later.

And, really, that's it.

Amazon.com is so simple it's dumb

This is good for you. Amazon.com is ready and capable to be your cash register. You don't need to know much about computers. You don't need to know anything at all about HTML or any sort of programming. Since there's no flashiness in the Marketplace, the playing field is level.

I'm here to show you how to improve your odds, taking advantage of the subtle little ways of getting attention and building a trade.

Entering the marketplace

Sit down at your computer, and cruise on over to ***www.amazon.com***. There is a strip of "folder tabs" depicted across the top. Over toward the left (probably the third in the row) is one helpfully marked **Books**. Click on that.

You are now looking at the main entry point for publications on Amazon.com – books, calendars, and general printed matter. You will be seeing much of this page, and will be feeling a lot of mixed excitement and trepidation when it pops up.

First, though, I'm going to make an excuse about my methods. Almost all pages on the Amazon site have long and complicated locations. One item I was looking at a few moments ago is located on a page that begins with

> http://www.amazon.com/exec/obidos/tg/detail/-/0761817867/qid=1073360557/sr=1-7/ref=s...

and just sorta trails onward from there.

Rather than expect you to type all that correctly into your browser, I'll be trying to direct you by a lot of "Click on this, then click on that" clues – it looks stupid, so go ahead and call me stupid but that's the best way to do things. Besides, the fine folks at Amazon.com, in their relentless efforts to keep things current and streamlined, change those pages once in a while, so all that typing might only get you a This page was not found result, while they've quietly changed the link to the revised location. We might as well take advantage of that coding. Here's a suggestion, though: create a folder in the Favorites or Bookmarks area of your Web browser, then tag the various pages that come up in our explorations – an address might occasionally change, but this would save you some digging in the meantime.

First things first: name & such

Before you set up a merchant account, you need to have a name. Catchy is good, and if you keep it as unique as you can, you leave yourself the option of expanding into trade that is semi-independent of Amazon.com, maybe your own website. This is the first step in creating what some businesses call a *public face*: what the world sees when they encounter your business.

Amazon.com doesn't allow you to be very creative with the presentation of this name. It's all lower-case letters, digits, underlines, and little else. Some merchants use the name of their real-world store, others use an on-line name they already feel comfortable with, or perhaps just some version of their own name.

Since very few buyers will ever attempt to look up your business name, it doesn't *have* to be easy to type – technically it could be a huge string of random letters and digits. However, it should be distinctive, not easily confused with other businesses (especially others already selling on Amazon.com), and maybe even descriptive or indicative of the sorts of items you want to focus on.

If you've ever tried to set up a simple e-mail account with a major provider like AOL, you have some idea how difficult this can be. Remember, there are many thousands of people who have registered a "screen name" on Amazon. Be prepared to run a few variations past the machine before you hit one that's tolerated. Make up a list before you start plugging away. For instance, say you're interested in being **HardCover Book Place**. You could try **hardcoverbook**, or **hardcover_book_place**, or **hardcover_books**, for starters. Maybe **hard_cover** is still available. If you're operating out of North Carolina, you could try **hardcover_nc** or some other variant.

If you already happen to be an Amazon.com customer, *start a new account for business only!* Though there likely won't be any major repercussions if you blur the lines between your selling and your buying, any accountant or attorney will tell you that this is good common sense that you ought to practice at every opportunity. If you are planning on quickly having thousands of items available on Amazon, then you should also have a separate bank account for these transactions, rather than mixing it in with your personal purchases – or worse, with your checks for car payments and rent. Even though you'll likely never sell the business, keeping your records as though that's a high-priority goal makes for an excellent start down the road of good business practice.

Registration & money matters

Now you have your list of names, one of which will likely be available. Primarily, this gives Amazon a way of identifying all the data specifically related to your transactions. No, you're not quite ready to jump in yet – you still need to have a way for Amazon.com to actually give you money.

My company had a checking account already, with a VISA-branded debit card. I have to recommend this for making the whole operation simpler. You need a place for Amazon.com to transfer your profits to, and since every once in a while you will likely come across an item that you're pretty sure you can sell for more, being set to buy makes sense. Having a checking account with an attached debit card also allows you a way to track purchases you make for resale – very handy when you're rummaging around in real-world stores, because you'll need some way of tracking your cash flow, for figuring taxes at the end of the year.

When you sit down at the computer, make sure that you have one of your checks or deposit slips in front of you, along with your debit card. You will need to enter the routing number for your bank and your account. This doesn't always go perfectly – I managed to get this right on the third try.

The difficult part of the following procedure is getting to the appropriate page. If done correctly, you will only need to do this once for the entire existence of your business. This is definitely an area where I don't want you getting lost, so here's one of my infamous bullet-point lists:

- go to the Amazon.com home page. At the top-right (just after the YOUR ACCOUNT button), click on **HELP**
- since you're here for a specific purpose, click on the heading **for Selling at Amazon.com**
- this brings you to a page that contains almost everything that a Marketplace seller will ever need to know – I truly feel that you ought to read every attached page at least once, on

the off chance that it could spark a boost in your operations

- right at this moment, though, we know precisely what you need, so click on the bullet-point entry **Amazon Payments Help**
- next, click **Applying & Payments Basics**
- this is one of those pages that you must read – when you're done, click on **complete an application** under "Applying for Amazon Payments"
- you'll be asked to sign in on your Amazon account – since you are starting something new, I recommend stating that you are new to Amazon: enter the e-mail address where you'd like to receive notifications of your sales
- enter your name or the name of the primary contact person in your company – please don't mess around here, as Amazon might need to get in touch with you for something important – and a password for your account; while I am impressed with the security at Amazon (especially its internal firewalls that you'll hardly notice), you are being offered room for a good-sized password and, since this is a direct link to your bank, why not use it thoroughly? Though Amazon doesn't make as much a point of it here as do some other sites, I usually recommend (a) a minimum of eight characters, (b) a mixture of upper- and lower-case letters, and (c) at least two numeric digits, 0-9, scattered around – I don't know that the Amazon procedure accepts punctuation characters, or I'd recommend adding a few of those as well
- next, you need to enter your credit-card information – it's best if you fill in all 16 digits with no hyphens or spaces, and the name of the person this card is registered to; again, I've never had a problem sending this to a Visa-logo debit card issued by our bank
- the screen that follows is billing and contact information: if you're working out of an office or storefront, or a post-office box, then that's the info you want here, along with the way they can get in touch with your day-to-day

contact (and if you haven't already guessed, this gives the fine folks at Amazon more ways to find out if you're a real business or trying to pull a scam)

- when you click on the **Continue** button, you will be sent to a screen that still makes my heart speed up when I see it – yes, I'm a sentimental fool – because you are almost literally standing at the threshold of a new business, and it's a little like signing the lease for your first office. This is where you're offered the opportunity to review everything you've just entered, and to edit it as necessary
  - first of all, make whatever changes you want to your Amazon "nickname," because what you enter here will be how your business is identified for a long time
  - then, I strongly recommend that you read the Participation Agreement before checking the little box, because you are signing a binding contract with one of the most powerful businesses on the Internet: you probably ought to know what you're getting into
  - and it would be best if you enter your checking-account information right away, rather than trying to figure it all out later – never argue when you find a streamlined place in any system – so check the box before "Enter my checking account information now"
  - click the **Continue** button – if you've overlooked anything vital, it'll bounce you back to this page, with a note in red under the heading of the area you didn't do right
- if you've never translated the numbers at the bottom of your check, this final step might take you a few minutes before they're successfully validated: enter the routing number (your bank's identification code) and your account number as indicated, along with the name on the account, then click the button
- and, with the usual understatement, the screen

will tell you "Thank You! You have successfully set up your Amazon Payments account"

At this point, you now have a Marketplace presence, with a name that customers will recognize when they see your available items, and a way for Amazon to give you money.

Of course, you're not *done* yet. Next, we have to tie your Marketplace account to a bunch of other stuff.

Other stuff

If you have access to your own website or page, you could store a logo there, a piece of art or a photo that you want to associate with your business. Amazon.com allows you to call this into an About me page – again, this is part of your public face. The vast majority of customers will never go there… but if they do, you come across as a bit more professional, and little touches like this can tip the balance and get you a sale.

Don't swipe from somewhere else. Other peoples' photos or artwork are not fair game just because you can grab the link. Simple graphics programs (like Paint) and even some word processors allow you to put together a decent-enough logo to get started. Rather than come across as slapdash, though, set aside an hour or two to come up with something passably interesting, or find someone whose skills are up to the task. If nothing else, your Amazon.com Merchant account name in a distinctive font will likely look good on a colored background, and you might have space to work in a brief slogan in a simpler font. Some sellers feature their website address, others scan in a photo of their real-world store. As with your name, this is one of the few points where you have a little room for creativity, so you might as well make the most of it.

When you have the image uploaded to your page or site, make a note of the exact Internet address for the image itself, not the page it's on. Write this down, or cut-and-paste it to a word-processor file.

Whether or not you have a photo or logo handy and uploaded, you ought to do your About me page anyway. Assuming you've actually set up a Marketplace account, it's easy. At the top-right of almost every screen, you'll see a **YOUR ACCOUNT** button. Next page, off to the right, there'll be a box titled Auctions, zShops, and Marketplace – that's you, so click on the second choice, **Your seller account**.

The left-side column of this page begins with the Your Inventory section, and I hope that you make regular visits to monitor the information that this can provide. For the moment, though, scroll down, past Your Transactions and Your Account Settings. The final chunk will be Your Storefront and Profile. You can either go directly to the area by choosing **View and edit your Auctions About Me Page**, or stop to admire your business's handy control panel with **View your Member Profile** then click **View/Edit Your "About Me" Page**. Down toward the bottom of the About Me listings, there's a diminutive **EDIT** button that brings up a screen with plenty of boxes to fill in your information. If you have the URL of your graphic, paste that into Logo: and you're ready to go. All of this will be posted to your About Me page a few minutes after you click the **Preview** button at the bottom and then the **Submit** button at the bottom of the next page.

If you are doing some advertising elsewhere, you can send customers directly to your Amazon account. For instance, if your account is for **hardcover_books**, your subsite will be under *www.amazon.com/seller/hardcover_books*. Enjoy!

Welcome to the club!

Now that you've got all your vital information together, everything is in place for that big step: opening your store. From there, if you follow my advice, it's mostly money in the bank – happily, in your account.

Find the entry

You've got your seller account together, all tied into your bank account. The confirmation from Amazon.com has arrived in your e-mail, and you even remember the password.

This gives you the equivalent of an empty shop. Okay, it's a little bare at the moment – but it's *yours*. The next step is to start putting merchandise on those empty virtual shelves.

It's easy to run up a list of all your listed items, organized in various ways, and I'll show you later how to go about doing that. These lists, though, simply pull together your individual listings. To the customer, every item you put up for sale is sitting on a virtual shelf alongside other copies of the same book. Once in a while, a customer will be interested in seeing all that exists under your name. Almost always, though, they are digging out that particular title.

Amazon.com has some excellent search tools. When they added their **Search Inside the Book** and **Advanced Search** capabilities in late 2003, this leapt even further into the stratosphere.

The thing is, I've been working with computerized databases since 1976 – just because I can find something is no indication that a sane human being will have the same success.

In my experience, simply finding the correct (or at least the *closest*) entry on Amazon for an item you want to list can take five to ten minutes, and even longer with an often-published book. If you are going to come out ahead on a business with such a small profit margin, every second you save is pennies in your account. I'm going to show you some of the most effective methods, and a few shortcuts.

Remember, you can't just plop your listing down in some entry that "looks close enough" because there's no such thing as close enough: You're either exactly where you ought to be, or you're swallowing a compromise that might come back to haunt you. If you have a customer who's looking for a used paperback, then putting your Like New first-edition hardcover into the middle of the used paperbacks will probably lead not only to you being ignored by *that* customer, but to you losing potential sale for browsers looking under (duh) the hardcover edition's entry. Don't be a bigger dork than absolutely necessary, especially when you can measure the habit in lost dollars.

The lazy way

I hate barcodes. When they're stuck onto books, my dislike can become quite passionate. Barcodes are inherently ugly, rectilinear scars upon some excellent cover design, and to top it off are far larger than they really need to be since they were designed for the scanners of thirty years ago.

But standardized code numbers are your friend when you're trying to make a buck by moving books.

There are now two ways to jump into rooting out a book by its numeric code. In either case, enter the number without spaces or hyphens.

- when you are in the Books section of the site, the "Search" area at the top offers an **Advanced Search** link, to the right of the two boxes and the **Go!** button. Click on this, then enter the item number you have.
- or, you can scroll down to the bottom of the Amazon "Welcome" page. Look for the centered block of keywords just above the "Bottom of the Page Deals"; off toward the right, there should be the words **Sell Items**. Click on that, then at the next page, click on the selection for Marketplace. This will put you at the Sell Your Stuff page, which has a format that is going to become a small but important part of your life. All you have to do is type in an identifying number for the book, click **"Start selling"** (or press enter), and pray that it's been entered correctly, if at all. (Yes, there are occasional mistakes here. One of the many corrections I've submitted was to fix a faulty ISBN for an entry, an error that led to extra work for us. Later, I'll briefly show you how the correction process works, and why it's good to spend a few minutes fixing things.)

Let's look at some of the different numbers you might be able to use.

ISBN

Nowadays, most books have an ISBN, an International Standard Book Number. If your book was published before the late 1970s, you might be out of luck as far as convenient numbers.

The ISBN might be available on the cover. It could be part of the barcode block, along the spine on the front or back cover, down the spine itself, or possibly between the publisher's name and the price. If the cover lets you down, you can likely find it on the copyright page. The ISBN existed before barcodes, though some publishers certainly seem to have been ashamed of it anyway, so check with care and save yourself some time.

Hyphenation varies, but the modern ISBN is ten digits long, and might end with an X – this is a digit, and must be entered if it's there.

Over the next few years, everyone is transitioning to a 13-digit ISBN, which effectively makes millions more unique numbers available; you are already seeing these on new books. This will make no big difference to you unless you buy some fancy software that is only set up for the ten-place version. If your merchandise is previous to 2004, you might never notice the change.

UPC

To the casual customer, a barcode is a barcode. However, books are often sold at places other than bookstores, and must therefore have a number that lines up with the system used for all the other merchandise. That number is the Universal Price Code, or UPC.

Some publishers handle the difference by putting the ISBN on the back cover, then printing the UPC on the inside of the (usually front) cover.

When you look at a UPC barcode, there are numbers printed below it. In most cases, you'll see two five-digit blocks. Don't leap to conclusions, though: unlike the ISBN, the full UPC number includes the single digits on either end, meaning that the common format is actually a twelve-digit number. Again, when searching Amazon on the basis of this number, don't enter any spaces or hyphens, just the digits.

The UPC is more likely to change during a book's

publishing history than the ISBN, so don't be surprised if Amazon can't find that particular UPC. Most small publishers don't use a UPC at all. Remember: this is merely a shortcut, and you may have to resort to searching by title and author.

Older codes

In the 1960s and 1970s, there were a few attempts at creating a system to identify every book. Some of these are very obscure, but if Amazon.com has the number associated with an item, you may be able to search for it. You might, though, need to be creative – again, maybe it's faster to search by other data, but if you are dealing with many items from a certain era, this could be a handy shortcut in your repertoire.

I have a 1974 paperback sitting in front of me, a first-print mass of Raymond Gallun's *The Eden Cycle*. According to Amazon, its ASIN is 0345242556, and I know from other searches that its ISBN is 0-34-524255-6 – one of those unusual situations where the numbers actually match up.

According to the book itself, its SBN is 345-24255-6-125. The SBN was a short-lived attempt at standardized coding, and had elements of both the ISBN and the UPC. The first nine digits became the last nine of the ISBN. The final three digits indicate the retail price, which is $1.25 – in the days when I was paying around a buck for a new paperback, and rarely more than two, having three digits was adequate – just as some versions of the UPC clearly bear an item's price. If you encounter an SBN or similar code, compare the number to its printed SRP and, if nine digits remain other than the price, put a zero at the beginning and try searching it. Any further effort, though, is probably fruitless for our purposes. Give it up, and try the following.

The power-search

Though I struggled at first, I've decided to be a fan of the **Advanced Search** feature. Before it was installed, I was able to simply enter part of the author's name or a few significant words from the title, and momentarily have a short list of likely entries that I would narrow down. I happened to go looking for one of my old favorite books the day the new features went in, and I was shocked to be told that Amazon had some 12,650 or so books that matched my request. I had run a search of three words, and the new software had diligently (and with blazing speed) applied its **Search Inside the Book** feature, proudly presenting every book that had those three words scattered throughout its excerpt. That feature is surprisingly fast and powerful, and I expect to use it increasingly for my personal research. However, for what you need as a merchant, it's almost entirely useless.

For you, the real usefulness is in the other new feature. When you go into the Books area of Amazon, there is a Search area toward the top of the screen. Don't enter anything in the boxes, but click on the words **Advanced Search**. This will take you to a screen with plenty of boxes for you to enter searchable information like author name, title, subject, ISBN, or other data. If you have that ISBN, it'll pull up the exact book almost every time. As I'll discuss later, though, you may do better to get a feel for other editions of the book (or CD) that you have, since that particular release might be ridiculously overpriced while there are plenty of copies available of other versions. You don't have to type out the complete title and name of the author – I'm so lazy that I often just type the last name and two or three main words from the title – but make sure that what you do enter is spelled correctly or the Amazon software will just route you to a "that item is not listed" page.

Though Amazon (and its users) are very diligent about hunting down errors, I've found dozens of items listed under amazingly incorrect or misspelled information. Until we get all those pesky bugs eliminated, Advanced Search has made things significantly easier for buyer and seller alike.

Find your center

Many times, if you search out an item on Amazon.com, the system will return a single entry to you, even though that book or CD has gone through many editions and reissues. This usually isn't a mistake: that single entry is probably a central point for all versions that have entries. Amazon has put some effort into linking them together; this is not as easy as it sounds, because misspelling of authors and titles effectively hides some entries, but when done well it sometimes pulls up editions that would not have appeared under a more direct search.

Generally, you can look up an entry, scroll down to the

Product Details area, and find the offer to show you other editions of the same title, sometimes with an **All editions** option if (surprise!) more than one version of the item has been published. You don't usually need to go any further: there might be only one entry, there might be a dozen or more. Because someone was diligent enough to make the proper linkages between entries, we have sometimes been able to correctly place an item despite terrible misspelling of the title and utter mangling of the author's name (for which, of course, we submitted corrections). This isn't perfect – if the title was originally misentered, you may have to drag it out by brute-force searching of everything published by the author – but you'll only have to dig further once in a while.

Be cautious about the times when there will be a Product Details link that says **All in-print editions**. We haven't tested this thoroughly, but we're concerned that using this feature might ignore Amazon listings for long-out-of-print versions – which is more than half our trade. Taking the label too literally can sometimes get you in trouble, too, as we've spotted more than a few times where an edition from the 1980s (long defunct before the birth of Amazon) was thought to be "in print." If it's the only choice you have, use it, but remember that you might not be getting the whole accurate catalogue.

While we're here, I'd like pause a moment for you to re-read that previous paragraph. This may look like a minor point – and, in the greater scheme of things, it is – but I can't emphasize enough that getting ahead in a crowded, competitive marketplace demands attention to detail and complete communication. And two words that could accurately describe the Amazon Marketplace are *crowded* and *competitive*. That's part of the fun!

More recently, those ever-amazing people at Amazon have made an effort to include brief notes about alternative editions right near the top, noting the format, retail price, Amazon price (if the item is currently available), and its availability on the Marketplace. This is a boon for the shopper who wants an at-a-glance idea of what's available, but it might not be exhaustive enough to really assist you as a seller. On the other hand, they're doing some of your footwork for you, since you can sometimes get a good snapshot of what your item is potentially worth in the greater scheme of things.

Narrow it down

If there are multiple editions listed, click on All editions and you'll get a results listing. Now you need to go low-tech and have a notebook or piece of paper, or open a new word-processor file. Make a list of the numbers in front of each entry. One at a time, click on the title to open each entry and determine whether it suits your item at all. If not, cross it off the list as a possible point to put your item. After all, if you place your paperback under the listing for an e-book (an "electronic book" file that is read with Adobe Reader or similar), your customer may never find your item. With books, most are clearly either Hardcover or Paperback (many times not differentiating between size formats), but more than a few say Unknown binding, or have no note at all. This might be incorrect, so treat it as strong evidence but look for more data. A "hardcover" might have the ISBN for the paperback you're holding, in which case I'd put the book there (and submit a correction). The Product Details section is very helpful, since it is at least a place that might provide you a correct publisher and publication date.

This isn't completely reliable for books, and is even less so for CDs. In researching one musician, I noted that ten of his CDs, released in the mid-1980s by a small company and *never* reissued, were listed as reissued by Capitol Records in 1998. I'm enough of a fan that I submit corrections every time I run across this sort of error. While not a major obstruction for you, be cautious about taking the information too literally.

Sometimes, you will not be able to find an absolutely correct entry for your item. A few months ago, I gave up when I could only find five entries, four of which clearly identified themselves as being for hardbound editions. The last was for unknown binding, so I set a price that was fairly representative of all available copies, and put our item there even though I couldn't make a match by ISBN. What struck me is that *all* available copies were paperback – at least my company doesn't look out of place.

A practice example

Here's a good one to try out, in order to get a little practical experience when you dive in.

From the Amazon homepage (the leftmost WELCOME tab if you're already at the site), look over at the leftmost column, where the fourth heading should be Books, Music, DVD. Choose **Books**. Click **Advanced Search**. On the next page, enter **berne** for Author and **games people play** for Title – these fields don't appear to differentiate between upper- and lower-case letters, so that's not critical. Click **Search Now**.

This is the best-selling book that Dr. Eric Berne published, and has been through quite a few editions and printings over the years. At the moment, I get a mere three Amazon entries (this fluctuates over time). Here's a good example of how you might have to sometimes dig awhile to find all the variations of a book you're trying to enter, as the three entries have the respective authors "Eric Berne," "Eric MD Berne," and "Berne M.D." If I enter "eric berne" on the Advanced Search page as the Author, only the first two entries appear. Be thorough in your digging; you may sometimes have to search for a misspelled version of the name. Many times, you can get around this by locating any listed book by the author, then clicking on the author's name on the page, which will then pull up every Amazon listing under that name, including misspelled or mis-entered versions – in this example, though, the listing for "Berne M.D." still doesn't appear.

We refer to the three that have appeared as *key listings* since some of them actually represent more than one listing. Here, the first one offers **See all (9)**, and the third one contains five more. When you request the nine, you get various versions, including paperback, hardcover, and large-print; with more recent books, you could get dozens of variations to cover audio books (tape and CD, abridged and unabridged), plus e-books and audio downloads.

In reality, I would never list this title unless it had some particular value as a collectible item. There are so many copies of it available for pennies on Amazon that it's not worth our time to go slogging through all the listings in order to find an appropriate "shelf" where it will probably languish among the other identical hundreds for months if not years. It is an excellent book, but millions have been produced, and the market remains saturated.

Note the prices

That reminds me of something very important, which we'll make use of soon.

As you are looking at the various entries, be sure to open up at least some of the **MORE BUYING CHOICES** new-and-used pages for the similar items. Many sellers have simply thrown their item into the first entry they stumbled over; some mislist an item in order to put it with a very expensive edition, where it will look like a bargain by comparison.

We found one where sellers were asking $12.95 and up for mass paperbacks mislisted with a $55 library-binding edition, instead of with the other masses where there were dozens available for $1 and less. I don't recommend this sort of dishonesty – it might net them an occasional sale from a less-than-diligent customer, but it's begging for a formal complaint to Amazon when that customer asks why they received a paperback.

Never intentionally confuse someone who has money to spend! All in all, it doesn't do anything positive for your business reputation, and can only come back to haunt you.

Look at the various new, used, and collectible items. If there are many, and especially if the lower tiers are clogged with *penny books* (the term we use to mean books selling for one cent, but it's become a generic for any item listed at far less than the Amazon shipping charge), then you could maybe take a moment to scan all copies available under that heading. Compare the descriptions to what you have in front of you – your slightly damaged item might be significantly better or significantly worse than most. Make a note as to the upper and lower limits you would put yours out at.

Again, there is no real amount of science here. You may struggle over your first listings, but soon enough you can scan a dozen entries as fast as it takes to open the pages, and an appropriate price will occur to you. We'll get into this in more depth over the next couple of chapters. For the moment, though, do your research and get a feel for the going price.

Be diligent –not obsessive

Only rarely will you have a book that is truly worth a whole hour of this sort of research. In general, the more valuable an item, the easier it is to find the proper listing. The books and CDs that are the most difficult for a Marketplace seller to accurately place and price are so common that you'll probably make only a few dollars. That is not a cost-effective use of your time!

Sometimes, rather than pounding your head against this wall, you need to be a bit arbitrary. Don't be outright lazy, but do set yourself some sort of time limit. For instance, after five minutes of narrowing your list of options, just grab one of the most likely, and go with that. Everything that I'm proposing here is about *improving* the chances of a profitable sale – not *guaranteeing* it. If I could promise you that following my hints would translate into a certain number of dollars within a certain number of days, then you'd have a fair reason to obsess… but I can't, and neither can Amazon.com, so don't fritter away your time.

Listing an item

Putting something up for sale is actually very simple. We'll get into the more complicated stuff of making a *great* listing later. For now, let's walk through the mechanics of the listing process.

Once you've located the Amazon.com entry for where you want to sell what you have, look over on the right. Off to the right of the item page is a bar marked MORE BUYING CHOICES. Below this is Get it for less! and the one you want: Have one to sell? Click on the **Sell yours here** button. There are other ways to get to this point, but this is by far the simplest and most reliable.

Category choice – caution!

On this page, you'll commit to whether you want your item listed as **Used** or **New** or **Collectible**. As new is new, you don't have any choice about condition – with few exceptions, anything less than perfect isn't new. For the other two choices, you'll be asked to state whether it's:

- Like New
- Very Good
- Good
- Acceptable

The first is literal: the item should be able to pass for a new, full-price item that you'd find sitting on a store shelf – some sellers call this *gift quality*.

For a book to be Very Good, it should have a nice cover and no significant internal markings, what we call a "gently read" book, or maybe a permanent stamp or marker line on the top or bottom edge of the pages that marks it as a lowered-price overstock item (this keeps customers and stores from returning it for full price when they bought it as a bargain).

To be merely Good, a book must be intact, not threatening to drop pages, with no internal marks that make reading difficult; many former library books fall into this category.

At the bottom of the heap are Acceptables; if you can make a valid case for Collectible status, you can get away with placing rattier books, because some collectors are overjoyed to have a half-decent cover or a "space filler" that completes a set until they can get a proper copy.

All in all, if a non-collectible book is missing a cover or pages, or is highlighted or stained to illegibility, Amazon.com doesn't even want you to list it, and I encourage you to consider dropping it in the trashcan (or at least giving it away to someone who'll appreciate it).

You can (and likely should) read the official Amazon definitions for each. Click the **Help** link (at the top-right corner of almost every page) to get to the general info page. Under "Selling at Amazon.com," click **Quick Start Guide**, then the hot-linked word **condition** in the bulleted sentence Describe the condition of your item and set your price.

(Now that I think about it, you probably ought to read everything selling-related at least once, if only that this will help you locate any gaps in your understanding.)

Be a little wary about the category you choose. With all other information you'll enter next, you can easily make changes when you relist an item if it hasn't sold within 60 days. If you decide to change categories, though, you will have to re-enter the entire listing. Not a major problem, but it slows you down, and your time is valuable.

Describing the item

Next, you're asked to describe your item in 200 characters or less. Many sellers enter little or nothing here. Generally, that's stupid. As you'll see in the following sections, a good description is usually what sells your item. Still, nothing requires you to do anything with this. If you're selling a fairly common book as New, and you have it under the appropriate entry, there's really not much reason to enter anything.

When you're satisfied with your entry, click the **Continue** button at the bottom of the page. The top of the next page will show you how your listing will look. This very handy, especially when you've run past the 200-character limit. If you have second thoughts and want to make some changes, use the Back button on your browser to take another run at it.

Having made a good description, you next enter the price you want to get. For many items, Amazon's software might recommend a price. Setting a price for an item is mostly up to you, and more controlled by whim than by rules; you're free to list every book you have at $1.95 or $1,000, whatever the age, condition, or rarity, if that's what you want to do. In a later chapter, I'll show you some of the considerations, and how this should affect the price you want to ask.

The rest is simple, though your choices can either give you a market edge or get you into trouble. Let's walk through these.

Taking their money

Sometime in the future, there will be a chance for you as a Marketplace seller to choose payment methods that you'll accept. For the moment, you *must* accept Amazon Payments and *only* Amazon Payments. If and when this becomes more flexible, my company will still take only this option. You may decide otherwise, but I highly recommend that you do not take other payment methods unless you see sound business reasons, and I'd still suggest staying exclusively with verified systems like PayPal, BillPay, etc. (I have friends who sell on other sites like eBay, and they are increasingly accepting only verified e-pay methods, as it greatly speeds the sales cycle, eliminates payments "lost in the mail" or just forgotten about, and pretty much makes fraud impossible – the electronic payment method thus removes a lot of stress and anxiety from their business dealings.)

Sending stuff out

Then comes the choice of shipping methods you are willing to use. You have to allow for Standard shipping, of course. Unless you live near a busy post office, though (or the equivalent express mail service), don't even think about offering the Expedited Shipping option – my company is in a city with notoriously poor service, with our "overnight delivery" typically taking three days, and letters across town up to two weeks. Since we cannot trust the claimed expediency ourselves, we don't want to promise it to a customer.

If we could guarantee delivery, we would gladly take the option. I did a little polling, and found that Expedited delivery comes into its own in three situations: Christmas, college, and seminars.

The first one is obvious. The second came to my attention when someone with a campus address ordered a minor classic of American literature that is currently out of print. I was in a generous mood, and the item was just heavy enough that first-class postage cost all of a dime more, so we paid the difference. For that dime, we got an enthusiastic e-mail from the customer, that the book had arrived so quickly that she was able to make it central to an important term paper. We bought some excellent word-of-mouth for ten cents.

Seminars are much the same, though in the business, motivational, or self-help sphere. When a seminar instructor is suddenly overwhelmed by a bigger registration than anticipated, he sometimes finds that a key textbook is between printings and unavailable from his usual supplier, and that every store assures him they can get more copies "in a few weeks." If the seminar is in four days, and the attendees are paying hundreds of dollars apiece, the instructor doesn't want to disappoint. He will gladly pay the extra couple of dollars if you can guarantee that the book will be there before he starts his presentation.

In much the same fashion, the world is full of last-minute shoppers who only remember birthdays a few short days before the occasion. Again, a few dollars to let someone know you haven't forgotten them is a bargain.

Though expedited delivery might be more trouble than it's worth to you, International Shipping is a money-maker that a surprising number of Amazon.com sellers don't want to bother with. We once listed a book where there were dozens of others available, but we couldn't make the price significantly competitive, and were surprised when it sold within a week to a buyer in Hong Kong. When we scanned the listings, we saw that none of the others had that title at a competitive price *and* were willing to ship internationally. We figure that many of them are relying on their own postage meters, a method that works great when you want to simply set a wad of domestic mail out for the postal courier to pick up at your home or office, but doesn't work for odd packages – like international mail. My office is two blocks away from a U.S. Post Office station, so we don't have a problem.

However, if you're going to go international, be sure that you spend some time looking into the rules that apply. Depending on the country and on the items you are shipping, someone might be liable for customs fees or taxes (or both), and that will either be the seller or the buyer. Handling this incorrectly might cause problems for your buyer, such as discovering that they're expected to pay duties on the "bargain" they got from you. If these regulations are simply too complicated for you, then don't offer international shipping until you are absolutely ready to leap into it. Generally, it's not much more hassle than paying the extra postage – but make certain.

If you are fortunate enough to have easy access to dependable shippers, then by all means check both the Expedited and International boxes! Each adds a little profit motive, and makes the item available to a larger customer base, both of which are good for you.

The exception to the rule

There are still a few books that we don't send out internationally, and that is because they are large. Putting a pocket paperback into an international mailing envelope is one thing, as it's small and only weighs a few ounces; we might even add to our profit by sending it out for less than we're receiving from Amazon for the service. But when you have a large book, in hard covers or on glossy stock, you could end up losing a few dollars on buying a box, struggling to pack it securely, and then paying extra for its weight or size, or both. (This applies to Expedited Shipping as well.) If you want to go ahead with this option, at least try to factor your likely added cost into your asking price.

Last details

Finally, enter the ZIP code from which you'll be sending the item. Eventually, this will probably become vital to Amazon.com estimating cost of shipping more accurately for the sake of the customer; at the moment, it really doesn't mean much, but they want the information anyway, and it's a simple enough chore.

Click the **Continue** button at the bottom of the page, and you're almost done.

The next page summarizes all the information you've entered for your listing, giving you a good chance to decide whether you're happy with it. Also, Amazon.com shows how much they're going to give you when it sells, including the amount you'll be credited for the shipping options you selected. Some sellers print this off for their internal records, but my company doesn't bother. If you need to make changes, I recommend that you ignore the **EDIT** button, as it has occasionally resulted in a Page not found or That page has expired error I couldn't recover from, so use your browser Back button instead – this isn't critical, but it's faster and less likely to cause problems.

If you're satisfied with how it looks, click either of the **List item for sale** buttons (to the right, near the top and bottom of the page).

This sends you to a page that is anticlimactic. I mean, there ought to be some sort of TAH-DAAAH fanfare or something to signify another item entering the Amazon.com catalogue. All you get is the note at the top of the page that Your listing is now live! Other than that, this page gives you a very nice summary of your listing and the dollar amounts that will change hands when it is purchased – some merchants find it useful to print this out for their records, but we've not found it to be worth the effort. If you have more items to enter, this page also gives you the standard "Search for your item" boxes, and you're ready to begin again.

Your item will "go live" in some indeterminable number of hours. We've had items show up in the listings anywhere from twenty minutes to ten hours later. In fact, we sold one book within an hour of entry.

For your records, Amazon.com will send you a confirmation e-mail for every item you've entered, if you've selected that option for your seller account. Their system has been so flawless that we may de-select this in the future, but at the beginning it's nice to get that little bit of reassurance that the machinery has been paying attention.

Getting the edge, part I: describe your item

Now you have a merchant account with Amazon.com, and you know how to get your items put out before the world. Well, you and many thousands of other businesses, that is. You can improve the chances that *your* item stands out, gets noticed, and is the one that gets the money in rapid fashion. The key to your selling is to post the absolute best description you can manage, brutally honest yet enticing.

We're going to go into some serious detail about the listing you put up for every item. As demonstrated in the previous chapter, there's really not a whole lot to it – hey, a few mouse clicks, less than 200 letters of typing, a price and a ZIP code; how tough could it be? Yet that little handful of information can make or break not just a single sale, but your whole business.

This chapter is the not only the heart of the book, but the first key to founding an Amazon reseller that will be competitive from the very first item you put up. It's a long chapter, it's got enough detail that you probably won't be able to apply it all at first, and you'll have to refer back for your first few dozen listings. That's okay! Learn by doing, improve as you learn, then go back and fix stuff if you feel the need – it's surprisingly easy to revise on Amazon.com, so don't waste too much time worrying about errors.

Your item listing

If you are going to make a decent go at selling stuff, no matter what the medium or the item, you need to have good merchandise at good prices. (Both "good merchandise" and "good prices" are more flexible than they might appear at first, but we'll get to that later.)

Given that those two factors are reasonably true, you will

need a good reputation, or at least not a bad one. If word gets around that you are unreliable, people who would otherwise be customers will not buy from you unless you have something that really tempts them. In the long run, it is your satisfied customers who bring you repeat profit, whether from their own future purchases or from those who are influenced to seek you out on the basis of word of mouth.

The problem is, all that goodwill happens *after* a sale. This bit of wisdom doesn't do you much good while you're still trying to get established. You need to develop a list of satisfied customers. That is why all of your initial contacts with customers – not just actual purchasers but everyone who stops by to look at your merchandise – must be as solid and reliable as you can make it.

Some real-world stores only allow people in by appointment, or unlock their doors for a few short hours every week. Usually, those who have this as an option are selling high-end items, whether antiquarian books or unique jewelry or rare musical instruments. That, of course, probably doesn't include you.

Anyone who's ever run a retail operation knows that most of the people who walk through your door, even if it's just a curious passer-by taking a moment to scan your shelves, might well lead directly to your next big sale. A casual browser will mention your store in conversation, and a listener will make a mental note to stop by. Someone disappointed at your lack of Balzac might sneer publicly at your huge selection of Dickens, and next thing you know every hardbound copy of *Great Expectations* has gone out the door.

When you sell on the Marketplace, almost all of your customer contact is going to be through your limited little words-only listings. There are a few other means on Amazon.com to present a commercial presence that is uniquely yours, but these are still of restricted utility: to find them, a customer must actively seek them out, or each seller must somehow put a link before that customer (we'll look at this in the chapter "The Next Step Up" near the end of the book).

Your reputation, whether initial or ongoing, lies almost entirely in how you describe every item you list. To maximize this potential goodwill, you need to describe each item accurately and thoroughly, in an exceedingly finite space, using only words.

Basic descriptions

To maximize the utility of the tiny window you're given to describe an item on Amazon.com, you need to run the risk of leaving some customers behind. A knowledgeable description of a book, in order to be crammed into a tiny amount of screen space, must many times resort to jargon, obscure abbreviations, and general mangling of the English language. That's going to confuse a few folks who might otherwise be interested in purchasing from you, and some of those may wander elsewhere.

Rather than market to these people, your topmost priority has to be information, both in quality and quantity. You need to clearly express what you have, and bring the less knowledgeable ones up to speed. I'm going to violate that very rule here by describing what I mean... but I have the luxury of a few thousand *words* in this book, where a Marketplace description has barely a couple hundred *characters*.

Ravenscroft's Rules:

1. Be concise, within limits of clarity.

2. Clarify possible questions about format.

3. Deliver the bad news first, and trust in your customer.

4. You make more friends as a pessimist.

I'll cover all of these in greater detail as we go along, but I want to expand on point 4 right away, because it seemingly flies in the face of conventional marketing wisdom.

If you put out two identical copies of a book, with even the same price, but rate one as merely "Good" and the other "Like new," which one is going to delight a customer more? The fact is, most buyers will settle for having their expectations met, and will likely just grumble over an item that doesn't quite make the grade... but give a buyer a "Good" book that turns out to be "Very Good" or better, good enough to be a decent gift, and you may have earned yourself the trust of someone who'll remember you the next time your name shows up as a seller. Being a bit of a pessimist allows the customer to benefit from optimism, and you'll be the one who profits.

Only the best listings are good enough

A good description is an implicit contract between the seller and the buyer. If I list a heavily damaged book, and describe it fully and accurately, then the buyer has no basis to complain, "Hey! You sold me a damaged book!" If I have reason to believe that it was an honest mistake on the purchaser's part, I can arrange for a refund, with a return of the item if it's even worth the cost of further postage. However, if a dissatisfied buyer complains to the referees at Amazon, the listing from which the purchase was made can be pulled up, and the complaint dismissed as baseless. If I promise a spotless, as-new hardcover, then send a mangled paperback, I'm going to have to do some fancy explaining, and that's as it ought to be.

Between those extremes, there's a big gray area. If I say little or nothing about the book, then I'm practically begging for the purchaser to be disappointed. True, I might be selling it for a dime as "Acceptable" – a step below "Good" in Amazonese – but I've left open the possibility that the purchaser will develop all sorts of expectations. Any ire will not find a route for official redress... but the merchant's goal is to accumulate a gaggle of satisfied customers, and keeping them in the dark is a strategy that heads the wrong direction, period.

A good description not only builds *reasonable* expectations and touts the positives, but undercuts the formation of *unreasonable* expectations.

The Ravenscroft standard for book & CD listings

If only through example, my company's listings are (ahem) exemplary.

We love books, and we enjoy making a profit. Both of these are assisted by cramming the best information we can manage into a tiny space. If other sellers decide to follow along, then we are competing fairly to provide the best service to purchasers, which benefits everyone.

Typically, a book listing from our company contains:

- publisher (or imprint – or both, if this seems significant)
- year of publication
- format of the specific item
- edition (if significant)
- printing (if significant)
- significant oddities, negative or positive
- bad news
- good news

Here's a typical listing from us:

> Penguin (Pelican) 1957 mass PB 1st/2nd. Some rubs front/back. Corner curl top-front. Slight sunning of spine. No interior markings, text block bright & square.

My computer says that this listing comes in at 159 characters, meaning that I've still got 41 worth of finagling I could do. Our description points out that as a second printing of the first edition, this copy might be of some interest, and is probably in good shape for its age. Since it's likely flanked by similar listings, a shopper can make a snap decision as to who appears to be offering the best deal – ours might be a better copy, but how can a customer tell unless the sellers give them something to go on?

Making a great listing

There are two points at which skill is required in this little business: when you acquire an item, and when you describe it. Right now, we're going to look at the back half of this.

category & condition

I want to clarify a few terms, because we see their usage bent, broken, and ignored every time we look at a few Amazon entries.

Collectible means more than the word indicates. Technically, *anything* is "collectible" – a sump-hole collects water, but that doesn't make it worthy of a high price. When the fever of acquisitiveness takes over, some people get weird and begin hoarding trash because "It might be worth something some day!" The official Amazon.com definition of the category tries to clarify this, but few sellers seem to care. So, a few rules of thumb to aid the intelligent:

- old authors or topics do not denote

collectability. We're tired of seeing, for example, everything from Winston Churchill listed this way merely because (a) he's an historic personage or (b) he writes about history. Neither is all Shakespeare (or even most) collectible.

- I don't care how unusual you might think an item is: if it's on the shelf in the major stores, it's not yet a collectible, and likely never will be.
- if a book was only given one edition, then all copies are first editions. Unless you can claim at least pristine as-new condition, it's not any more collectible than anyone else's item.

If you're going to list something as Collectible, then make a little effort to explain and justify your decision. This, actually, is supposed to be an Amazon rule, but I've never heard of it being enforced. A seller gains no points with me when the title is still in its first edition and that's the entire basis of their used item's supposed collectability. It should be a signed or inscribed copy (but *not* a gift inscription signed by "Mom & Dad"), or contain promotional materials, or be a variant edition, or in a foreign edition that doesn't have its own entry, or something of that sort.

New is *new* – period. Don't look stupid by claiming "it was almost new when I bought it." If it doesn't look like it'd be appropriate on a retail-store shelf or rack, then it ain't new. We've seen stripped books – where the cover has been torn off and returned for credit – listed as New; I hope I don't have to point out to you how many ways this is not only stupid but illegal.

Like new books resemble items that have never sold but have been sitting on the shelves for a while. They might have slightly dented corners from being dropped, or some scuffing to the cover or dust jacket or bottom edge. Many sellers put remaindered books (the ones with the marker line across the edge) here if they're otherwise in perfect shape.

Our company's rule is: when in doubt, downgrade. You'll benefit more from underselling an item (or not listing it at all) than overselling.

publisher/imprint

Many times, a book has been through more than one publisher, maybe a dozen or more, yet Amazon.com only shows a single entry. Some clients don't want that edition, while others would pay a premium for it. Either way, pointing out clearly what you're offering leads to happy customers, even if they don't buy from you.

year of publication, edition, printing

This trips up a surprising number of amateur sellers, and sometimes someone with a great deal of experience.

Some publishers list the year they first published the book, nothing more, which leads beginners to say that a paperback with a big ISBN barcode on the cover is a 1959 first edition. (Vintage Books is a regular miscreant in this regard.) If you aren't absolutely certain, then you're better off saying **1980s** or **1985(?)** if that's your best estimate.

The same goes for the print run: just because the copyright page says "1st Grsmrgl Printing 1967" doesn't mean your copy was actually printed in 1967. If you're intelligent enough to be capable of reading my advice, then you're bright enough to make an educated guess as to the real information. Go ahead and act like the professional you want to be.

Sometimes, publishing information is extraordinarily detailed, though perhaps not obvious. Here's a minor secret of the publishing world. Many times, the copyright-notice page will display a bizarre line of text that encodes the very information of which I speak; I'll explain a few variants.

3 4 5 6 83 82 81 80

When this book was first printed by this publisher, the left end began with a 1, and the right with 78. Every time it went through a new printing, the printers literally went to the printing plates and scraped the first number off the left, and the rightmost number if the year had changed. The above translates as "third printing, 1980."

This is left over from a previous era, when a book's plates might begin degrading, depending on how many copies were produced, how well the plates had been treated, whether the best workmanship and materials had been put into their creation, and so on. Sometimes, a new plate was created as a copy of the old one, which renews the physical surface but also carries along any damage that has already taken place. Less often, the book might go into a new edition with some changes to content. Discovering which version was sitting on a store's shelf was made easier by some sort of tracking code, but this could be a bit idiosyncratic.

To cite a typical story, a publisher had ordered a new printing, to be sent directly for distribution. The printer was willing, but pointed out that the plates hadn't looked top-notch the last time around. The contact person at the publisher interpreted this as malingering, and probably a ploy to extract a nice sum for making new plates, and therefore ordered printing to go ahead. When customers opened the new books, they found masses of broken, spotty type. All copies were pulled from the shelves, easily identifiable from any older copies by a glance at the copyright page.

Though metal plates are hardly used nowadays, and even modern paper or plastic printing plates are discarded quickly, these tracking codes are still used, sometimes out of a sense of tradition, sometimes as a sort of luck-charm, in hopes that the book really will be popular enough to require a tenth printing.

1 2 3 4 5 6 7 8 9 F G B F G B 8 7 6

This is a variation on the previous example. As other information on this page reveals that the first edition in this form appeared in 1986, I'd be very safe claiming that this is indeed the first edition, from 1986. However, remember that many books go through exceedingly short print runs, and might get two or five or twelve printings in a single year if the publisher is worried about overstocking the demand. That leftmost number could as easily mean first *printing* as first *edition* – but, taken together, it's as safe to claim the latter than the former, and I'd be confident about listing it as "1st ed." I still have absolutely no idea what **F G B** means.

First Smootie Press paperback printing
July 2001

10 9 8 7 6 5 4

It's not unusual to see something like this listed on Amazon as "Stated first printing." It doesn't state anything of the sort; this is from the fourth printing.

9 8 7 6 5 4 3 2

First Edition

I like these people. The information is easy to interpret, and I'd enter it as "1st ed 2nd print" or "1st/2nd."

Greep & Wuu edition / June 1980

Flbrmph edition / April 1981

40 39 38 37 36 35 34

This is one of those things that gets the less-cautious in trouble. The book I'm looking at is the Flbrmph mass-market paperback. Many Amazon.com sellers would unhesitatingly say it's therefore obviously a 1981 edition. Well, yes and no: for the most part, when someone who truly knows books says "edition" in the strict sense, this means "the last time that noticeable changes were made." But don't look dumb by taking this so literally. A book can go through many years and many printings without actually changing edition. For instance, if someone handed you a nice new King James Bible, would you tell all your friends that you had a first edition? Therefore, rather than look silly when presented with this sort of information, don't even mention the edition, just the printing – at most.

Since the listed (or standard) retail price (commonly abbreviated **SRP**) printed on the cover of this item is $6.99, I wouldn't hesitate to list it as **1990s** or **1995(?)**, *possibly* adding **34th print**. You're doing this *not* to entice a buyer, but to inform them that it's nothing special, just a good read.

[Let me take you aside for a moment in a slight change of subject. Actually, my company probably wouldn't list this item at all. The number of printings alone makes clear that there are a million of the things wandering around in just this edition. As the particular author is very prolific, it's gone into a new edition since, with unifying covers for the series. Since it's a thriller, the sort of book you generally read only once, it's not even worth preserving. If I had a real-world store, I'd put it out for a dollar, maybe two. Instead of bothering to list it, this item will be passed along or donated.]

format

In general, it's just a nice idea if you fully describe a book's format, but you can also be practically forced into it. Sometimes, Amazon.com has the title listed, but only in the wrong format, so you might have no choice but to put your hardcover up for sale under the entry for a paperback, or a prestige trade with the mass market. And sellers are often lazy or clueless, and fill up the area with the wrong format – recently, we entered an item correctly, but noted that almost all of the copies for sale under the hardcover entry were mass paperbacks, and most of the copies under the paperback listing were hardcovers. You should begin by doing your research, and avoid looking as (let's face it) stupid as those sellers. If you're stuck, expend the few characters and tell your potential customers what you're offering – after all, saying "trade PB" takes all of ten letters from your 200, and that's a worthwhile investment.

The three main categories are hardcover or **HC**, trade paperback (**trade PB** or just **trade**) and mass-market paperback (**mass PB** or **mass** or **pocket**). Variation abounds, but try to be clear. Some old-timers will refer to a hardcover as **clothbound** or **cloth**, but this could get confused with some children's books that are actually in cloth softcover; if you've got an edition that's truly in **cloth boards**, or even **leather boards**, then say so, and mention the color too, because that's important to collectors. (Don't claim leather unless you're *certain* – a collector can get *very* upset over getting leatherette or embossed vinyl instead, and only ugliness ensues.)

For "coffee-table" books, you can say simply **oversize** or give the actual dimensions (for the most part, customers really don't care how thick it is, or how many pages) either in inches or metric – when you do this, squeeze the space and use a lowercase X rather than trying to enter a symbol, so you can refer to a mass as **4x7"**, though for odd sizes we commonly use centimeters rather than wasting space on fractional inches. Some titles have multiple trade editions in different sizes; taking a few precious characters to say **5x8** or **6x9** is appreciated, and might offer a browser *exactly* what they were looking for. Larger soft-cover books can be called **fullsize PB**.

If your item is an older mass, you can grab the attention of some collectors by just saying it's a **shorty**, as many pulp novels were much squarer in mid-century. Some trades have cover edges folded to resemble dustjackets, or bound soft boards, or extremely fancy printing or paper that doesn't appear in other editions; if it's not an actual limited-edition rarity (in which case you should just say that), then you should describe it a bit, at least to point out that you're selling a **prestige trade**. And if you have one of the current fad of "tiny" books but can't find the proper Amazon.com entry or the entry is deluged by the wrong format, make sure to mention that your item is a **mini PB** or **mini HC**.

I'd forgotten about this until recently: some paperbound books are actually sewn "signatures" of folded sheets, like good-quality hardbound but in soft covers. The publishers, in a brief fit of enlightenment, meant them to be read repeatedly over the years. You can be creative with this, but we list them as **sewn mass** or **sewn trade**. Trust your envisioned customers to understand why this is a good thing, and that you're offering an unusual item.

If your item is **large print**, don't list it with the rest of the books unless (a) there is no large-print listing for that title, and (b) you clearly make this distinction. I've tried to read such books when there was no other edition available, and I felt as though EVERYONE WAS SHOUTING AT ME. Besides, large-prints generally sell for more, because they're less common, and customers who prefer larger print will actively search for those listings.

I think it's time to set aside terms like **folio**, **quarto**, **octavo**, etc. Back when the phrase "a standard sheet of paper" actually meant something, these terms each referred also to standard dimensions. On Amazon.com, though, I think you're just confusing the great majority of potential buyers, and there's really no good means nor need to educate them. For what it's worth, a full-size hardbound book is roughly octavo (**8vo**), a mass paperback is a sextodecimo (**16mo**), and a coffee-table book is quarto (**4to**, but I've seen **qo**).

Though it's not our focus here, I want to mention *audio books*. Foremost: always, always, *always* describe your item fully. I spoke with another seller who can't sell her high-priced ten-CD sets because the entry is inundated with people selling the three-cassette version – the former are unabridged from the text, the latter are heavily trimmed, so she (not unreasonably) charges more. I told her to revise her listing to clarify this so that her pristine $25 sets weren't competing with all the $1 ex-library tapes. And, for heavens sake, don't sell cheap knock-off copies – if you feel compelled to violate a whole slate of federal and international laws, then you ought to have the brains to do so on a streetcorner rather than at an Internet site where the managers know, at the very least, your bank account number.

oddities

There are dozens of things that pop up to make an occasional item unique. We listed four paperbacks, editions of widely printed classics and rather common, but they each had covers that tie them to a contemporary movie or television program. Another had a newspaper clipping of the author's obituary, put there by a previous owner. I have shamelessly asked an occasional author to sign a good older book. (There are even services that will do this for you, one of which charges between $5 and $25 to take charge of pestering the author! As the author gets a cut, they're usually quite happy to do this, and take an afternoon to autograph a case of books.) I once owned a book that had been marked up for a new edition by the author, who had signed a note to his editor inside the cover. I have even seen a book that was inscribed (to a friend) by the person to whom the book was dedicated. If you are going to list a book as Collectible, such fillips corroborate your claim, and should be noted.

Don't forget the potential for "sentimental value": we listed three different editions of one book, all with very distinct covers, one of which we described as "the awful salmon pink" – somewhere, someone might want to replace the version they once owned.

We have also pointed out the cover artist or illustrator, because that is of interest to some collectors: Edward Gorey handled the typography or internal illustration or cover art of many books, others seek out science fiction novels for which Leo and Diane Dillon contributed their amazing cover paintings, and Richard Powers also has a following.

Once in a while, a book has been published under multiple titles but only one listing appears. The book on which the movie *The Russians Are Coming! The Russians Are Coming!* was based was reissued briefly under that title, but is only listed on Amazon as *The Off-Islanders* (by Nathaniel Benchley, in case you're curious), which is where we put our item.

Occasionally, too, the Amazon.com entry mangles the title or the author's name, or both. While this is a pain, do your best to dig up the proper entry for your listing, then submit corrections to improve the chances of being found by potential purchasers.

bad news about condition

The following is by no means a definitive list, but contains some of the more useful notations that we've assembled, most of which will inform a book fan without unduly confusing the average buyer. Some of these are quite idiosyncratic to us. (If you want to learn more about the art of valuing a book and describing its condition, there are some good references out there. I recommend *The Official Price Guide to Collecting Books*, by Marie Tedford and Pat Goudey, as a great place to start.) Rating a book is far more art than science, but you can pick it up rapidly with practice – be sure to swipe from other listings if they use a term that you instantly grasp, because your ideal potential customers pick up on these terms, too.

major or **severe**: easily noticeable damage that almost threatens the readability or physical integrity of the book. Knocks its quality down two or three notches (an otherwise Like New book can hope for no more than Good, and is probably merely Acceptable).

moderate: "second-look" damage that doesn't leap out at you but still clearly cuts into the value. The sort of thing that pushes listed quality down at least a step.

minor or **light** or **superficial**: no big thing, but hovers at the edge of making a book less-than-new. For instance, dents on the cover that are only apparent under a good light.

mild: some sellers (like us) use this to indicate that our keen antiquarian eye has noted something and we want to be absolutely honest, though the average buyer might never notice it. Mild damage is generally the sort of thing a restorer could fix in seconds.

tiny: less than half a millimeter, or almost no occurrences.

small: less than five millimeters, or few (but noticeable) occurrences.

some: significant and hard to miss, but not overly disruptive.

large or **much**: so obvious a problem that it knocks the item down a grade or two by itself.

even: not limited to one portion. Usually describes yellowing, spotting, soil, fade, etc.

overall: a more pessimistic take than **even** (unless attached to something positive like **solid**). For example, **overall wear** sets a different tone from **even wear**.

spine break: a bend across the book that breaks the spine glue, tears open a cover (maybe both), and probably creases most or all of the pages at the binding. A particularly bad break can result in the spine being snapped into two visibly separate parts.

spine bend: less severe than a break but still affecting the overall shape. You see this when a paperback has been carried in someone's back pocket. In many cases, it's the only flaw.

spine bow: a more even sort of bend, running a significant length of the spine.

spine crease: a fold down the middle of the spine face caused by the book being opened, and a part of normal use. A collectible paperback with an uncreased (**flat**) spine is generally desirable, though many books leave the printer with some spine creasing caused by the binding process. If you're not pushing a book as collectible, don't worry about it as a negative attribute unless the creasing is so deep as to diminish the legibility of the title.

spine split: when a spine crease goes particularly deep in a paperbound book, either from being forced open or from poor glue, the pages will take sides. If it is not further abused, this isn't usually difficult to repair, though it's not worth having done professionally for a fairly common book. If otherwise collectible, this is no big thing, but it definitely cuts into the value of a reading copy.

spine off: older books (whether paperback or hardbound) and those that have seen rough handling might lose the strip of cover material on the spine. If you don't have it, then be honest and say something like **spine off/gone**.

spine free: the spine strip is partially detached. Again, if preserved on a collectible book, this *might* push the value down one grade, but it definitely drops the value of a reading copy one or two grades.

read crease: definition varies, but using the term gives a good general idea of the damage. Imagine holding a paperback open with both hands; if you push your fingers in harder, bending the covers slightly around your fingertips, you create one sort of read crease. If the centers of the cover edges have rounded dents, this might be called **thumb crease**. What many sellers call a read crease we describe instead as **crease at spine**, where the cover is pulled back far enough to fold it slightly near the binding edge.

handmark: some sellers use this to mean read creasing; we mean the pattern of stain and soil at the spine and sometimes at the cover's leading edge caused by sweaty hands

stain: a significantly discolored blot, like coffee or grease.

soil: usually refers specifically to cover discoloring. What is called soil can look at first glance like sun-damage darkening or browning, but generally has a coarse texture. This is usually simple to clean, but we decided that the extra profit we'd make wouldn't be worth our time.

lean: a common problem with big books, though I've seen it on slim papers. If a book is left standing free on a shelf or with weight on it that skews the covers in relation to each other, then it takes on a lean. Hardcover books can pick this up as the **hinges** (the softer cloth holding the covers to the spine assembly) soften due to use and age.

sag: when a hardcover sits upright on a shelf, the page

block tries to fall downward since the cover is slightly bigger. If it goes far enough, the bottom of the leading edge will end up shelfworn, especially in the center pages. Also called **droop**.

warp: when the book (in part or whole) is no longer flat. Paper has a grain, and moisture will make it expand in one dimension more than another, which works out even less well when one edge of that paper is glued and therefore unable to stretch. Some paperbound books come from the printer with a noticeable warp. We've described a few books as **wavy** because the warp didn't make one big "cup" so much as a series of smaller ones.

rounded: can mean a few things. Rarely, it refers to the book being less than flat. Most of the time, it means the spine is no longer flush and square due to having been held open. In an older paperback, might mean the corners of the leading edge have been gradually chipping away and they're far from sharp.

fly: the flyleaf of the book, the pages before the title page, as in **Owner name on fly**.

title: the title page of the book, as in **Pencil notes on title**.

stamp: short for rubberstamp. Could indicate anything from a numbered distribution mark across the top (**head**) of the book (since many mass paperbacks showed up at stores with this, it shouldn't cut into a book's value, but leave that call to the buyer), a company stamp (usually meaning it's been an overstock item), a bookstore's stamp inside the cover or on the fly or title, or the stamp of an owner or library. Use your judgment, but usually a great deal of detail isn't needed: **Store stamp inside-back cover**, **Owner stamp fly**, **Foot remainder stamp**, etc.

ex-library: this covers a lot of territory! Give some idea of how extensively stamped it is, how much damage was done by glued-in card pockets and circulation notes, how extensively it's been repaired with tape, stuck-on labels, and so forth. If the DJ is in good-or-better condition and carefully sealed under Mylar film, make that a positive point.

sticker: mention type and location. A store's price sticker on the cover is easier to forgive than a dozen Smurfs on various pages. Some stores and distributors cover the ISBN with a UPC barcode if that's what their computers work with.

taped: libraries and owners tape spines or edges to repair damage or to minimize wear. Some are very professional, others quite poor. Mention location; if it's particularly ghastly (like electrical tape, or gift tape printed with holly leaves), mention this apologetically.

adhesive: stickers and tape fail with age, but can leave gummy residue. If you have a high-end book, you may want to make a cautious effort to maximize value by removing this... but it takes practice, and wrong choice of solvent or method could cause more damage than good. You may do better to inform, and leave well enough alone.

blotted: some used-book shops, overreacting to fears of customers who might accuse them of overcharging, black the printed price out with marker; they might go so far as to put black blots over the prices on both covers, the spine, the ISBN, and even inside the book. Mention this at least as **price blotted**.

effaced: the aforementioned merchants might instead use a ballpoint pen, pencil, or knife to mark out the price from the cover, damaging the board and even taking off a small chunk.

peel: sometimes the surface of a cover loosens (delaminates) with age and wear, usually around the edges but occasionally at the middles of the spine or leading edge due to hand dampness and flexing.

curl: especially at corners, but also along the leading edge, the cover might begin to lift away from the rest of the book. If the printing was less than perfect, even a new book could have corner or edge curl.

turn: we use this to denote a more overall bend that is limited to a portion of the book. For us, **turned corner**

means that the book no longer lies absolutely flat but that this hasn't resulted in creasing of the pages or cover.

bend: more severe than a cover curl, possibly creating an irregular wrinkly line where it's most severe, but not enough to break through the inked surface or the paper fibers on the back.

crease: an actual line where it's obvious that the page or cover has been folded entirely back and even pressed down. Cover creases also appear from placing heavy objects on the book. A **cover crease** is seen as more significant than **creased pages**.

fold: we use this occasionally because some cover creases don't significantly mar the book, but the board is weakened and might never again lay flat.

hole: damage that goes completely through a cover, or damage inflicted to a CD case's edge or corner or over the barcode to mark it as discounted.

punch: a neat hole, used by some distributors to indicate that it's a discounted or remaindered book, and by some used-book sellers to remove the printed price. Sometimes called a **drill**, especially on remaindered CDs.

cut: refers either to thin, neat damage inflicted by a sharp edge (scissors, or overly enthusiastic knife-wielding when unpacking), or sawing into the edge of a CD case to indicate remaindering.

clip: a reseller might cut off a corner of the dustjacket where the retail price was printed, which we just call a **price clip**. Unscrupulous sellers clip the corner that says "Book Club Edition" and try to sell it as a rarer commercial hardcover. Some owners of much-read paperbacks lop off the corners of covers and pages as they curl and fray. In any case, mention the damage along with a guess as to intent.

gouge: damage that has broken the printed surface and possibly taken some of the board. Whether large or small, make an effort to give indication of size.

dent: damage that isn't quite so alarming as a gouge. We use it to indicate small indentations or lines in the cover that don't break the surface.

scuff: wear that has taken some of the shine off of a paper cover's surface or marked the material of a hardbound. Indicate its depth or severity.

ding: generally, indentations anywhere on the book. We usually describe such damage to cover edges as just dings, and to some or all of the pages as an **edge ding**.

chip: the printed surface is breaking off the paper stock in small flakes. A common problem of paperback covers, especially along the edges. Some new books suffer from this due to being cut to size by the printer, or because of stress along the spine. Buyers aren't put off by a few missing flakes that are less than a millimeter, but this can get quite extensive as the edges soften with age and use. The spine area is especially prone to chipping. This also refers to dustjackets that are beginning to show age. Give an idea of its extent, and whether any such patches are significant.

dogear: some owners mark passages by folding the page corner over. With age, these can become very brittle; you may be better off to just leave them alone. We list a few books as **Some dogear** to indicate that it affects more than one page.

chew: just what you might think. We see a few books that are in pretty good shape, except for corners or edges that clearly show canine or feline dentition. Make some effort to describe the extent of damage.

spot: can indicate anything from small spattered stains to a few drops of water, or even mildew. Mention location and extent.

mildew: if you know what this looks like, then by all means mention it – and isolate this item from the rest of your inventory! I've cleaned up a few items that had *dead* mildew infections, using a very soft eraser. If you have an item that is infected but otherwise good, spray it *lightly* with something like Lysol, then stuff it into a plastic bag for a few days, and accept that the propellant might damage the cover; if it's otherwise damaged, and not clearly collectible, save everyone some trouble and throw it away. Mildew is second only to bookworms (which, thankfully, I haven't encountered in many years) as a major transmissible disease of books, and can quickly eat the paper. Inform the buyer clearly if this is a risk.

water: could be anything from overall warping to individual malformed pages, or pen underlines that have become blots. Clarify when you use it.

fox: brownish spots that usually mean the paper is rotting. You probably ought to avoid using this term, as you can be easily more specific, but you'll encounter it occasionally, or as **foxed** or **foxing**.

sun: a general term for damage caused by prolonged exposure to sunlight. Actually, much **sunning** is just a matter of age. Usually a combination of fading and yellowing; when you say **Sunned spine**, people seem to get the idea. Page edges and tops sun, too, so mention whether this has darkened the paper color or faded a colored edge.

fade: lightening of color due to age, light, or other factors. Some color combinations of text and background can fade out to an indecipherable off-white.

discolor: a more general-purpose term for fade, soil, yellow, etc., without being so straightforward and localized as staining. The term is useful when listing details of all the possible causes would beat a dead horse; when you use it, you're throwing in the towel, but be sure to emphasize any particularly *good* points.

highlight: the result of using brightly colored felt-tip markers to note significant passages. Our listings start at **no highlight**, ramp up through "light" then "minor," and peak somewhere around "heavy" and "extensive." If it only affects a chapter, or a few pages, say so.

marg: easier to spell than **marginalia**. Signifies notations in the white space around the edge of pages. Once in a great while, if you can demonstrate the provenance (history of ownership) of the book, you might have a rarity: the handwritten notes of a famous person. Almost every time, though, it's random doodling of a student, and brings the value down a notch or two.

lined: underlines and circles on the pages.

soft: some book materials become more flexible and cloth-like with age. Covers, boards, cloth, and hinges can begin to soften, which might be heading toward fragility and collapse. Edges and corners can also soften, which is not just a sign of wear but indicates that the process is continuing, on the way toward becoming **round**.

crisp: some papers, and especially those used in cheap mass-market paperbacks a few decades ago, retained sulfur from the bleaching process. With time and moisture, this turns into acid that eats the paper; it becomes **brittle**, especially at the edge, and even cautious handling causes the paper to break. Corners and edges flake away, and sometimes these breaks can intrude far across a page, breaking off a chunk.

fragile: would probably disintegrate if treated like a newer book. This can apply to paper, covers, binding, or the overall book. The fragility can be due to anything from paper deterioration to crumbling glue.

yellow: this isn't indicative by itself, but informing the buyer is a good idea. The paper might have been a bit on the yellowish side to begin with, or the edges could be actively breaking down. You have leeway to say things like **even light yellow** or **some edge yellow**.

brown: serious yellowing, likely on the road to crisp.

Be sure to mention anything, however odd. If the book seems to have been the victim of melted chocolate, mention this prominently. The same goes for smelling terrible (**moldy** is adequate for a whole range of odors you don't want to think too hard about) or having the cover art partially stripped away by some solvent.

good news about condition

Don't hesitate to describe the book as though it's made up of components. We list books that have terrible covers, but **pristine** interiors. Be utterly honest about the flaws… but apply some tasteful superlatives when they're warranted. The good attributes of a book are easier to describe briefly. Here are a few of the terms we've found especially useful.

not: your single most powerful word! Attach it to the best one or two attributes of the book: **Not remainder, No marks**, etc.

intact: this makes clear that, though the item may be torn up and falling apart, all the pieces are attached. This is especially important to collectors, who may be happy to restore a fragile book they got a good price on.

complete: all the pieces are there, though maybe not stuck together. Give an approximate percentage to help the buyer decide. Shoot a little low; a dust jacket that's missing a golfball-size corner could be called **90% complete**, and a completely gone end-flap makes the **DJ 70% complete**. Try to describe what's missing.

solid: really means nothing more than an all-in-all physically good copy. Implies that, while it might not look the greatest, it's a long way from going into the trash.

tight: a new book resists opening because the binding is fresh and the materials haven't relaxed yet. Some books, if treated well, will have this feel for many years despite handling. I listed a paperback older than me that was tighter than most of the new books I'd bought for myself. This implies that it's got years left before the pages loosen from the spine. If your hands tell you it feels much newer than it is, then call it tight.

bright: usually means that the paper isn't yellowing; more generally, the type is crisp and easy to read.

square: the book has not shifted in any manner, and the spine has not taken on a curve, so it overall has straight lines.

sharp: we mean the edges and corners are unworn by

reading or shelving damage, and might say so if we have a little extra space in a listing. Some sellers apparently use this as a synonym for "pretty," and I don't recommend it.

light pencil: if you can claim this, then use it. Non-permanent marks that don't deform the paper can be removed easily by an owner, though it might not be worth your time to do so yourself, and you would also run the risk of damaging the paper or the print.

no highlight: we mention this as a feature because lack of highlights is very important for a student buying a textbook – even if it's not in the greatest of condition.

good read copy: makes clear that, while the item might not be choice as a gift or collectible, it's more than adequate as a book.

Setting the price

This topic really ought to go right about here, but the information is so vital that I wanted to make sure it got proper attention. So, you'll find it in it's own chapter, immediately following this one.

Stupid things to avoid

For each item you list, you can take 200 characters to describe what you've got and entice a potential buyer. If it wouldn't get me in trouble, I'd simply lift some quotes from the Amazon.com pages. But because some are very common, I can paraphrase shamelessly – and, worse, not only are most of these the entire listing, but the same stock phrase is used by the seller in dozens of listings. Compare the following to the Ravenscroft Standard:

FREE UPGRADE TO 1ST CLASS

> If this seller has a huge name-recognition value, and is implicitly trusted to send out flawless items, the freebie is worth talking about... but wouldn't those trusting customers already know that? This just indicates laziness.

> Our customer's know were fabulous look at our ratings baby!

All I'm really certain of is that someone knows how to spell "fabulous" – and that may be a fluke. Try telling me something about the item.

> This book is so great we should just keep it.

Every time I see this one – yes, they used it in dozens of places – my immediate response is, "I agree!"

> size: 16mo, dust jacket: none as issued, condition: missing

Trivia Master says: I find this deeply disturbing. The size is printer shorthand for "sextodecimo," nowadays largely meaningless but once indicating that a standard sheet of paper had been folded in half four times to make 16 leaves of a finished book. Here in Reality, it's used to indicate a pocket-size book, almost always a mass-market paperback. That's good because, of seven entries for this title on Amazon.com, this is the only one for a mass. Therefore, the subsequent notes are not only pointless but rather weird: can something that's never existed be missing?

> DIFFERENT BOOK

Okay, yeah, I get it: sometimes you have a really nice book, there are twenty-seven titles listed for the author, and the book you have isn't one of them. You succumb to temptation and list your book in the Marketplace entry of a different title. (We have more than a dozen books that are nowhere to be found on Amazon.com, half by very popular authors, and we keep them in a box in hopes that they'll be reprinted someday.)

There's not much likelihood that a potential buyer searching for that very title will look everywhere. Are you going to be so foolhardy as to list that single item under every book by the author? If you do go ahead and put a listing in more than one place, three or more orders for the single copy you've got could only lead to embarrassment.

Don't be dumb

I don't know who would buy on the basis of those listings, but for those in danger of being swayed, I will sum up this chapter very briefly:

1. Don't waste a customer's time.
2. Don't make it clear that you don't care.
3. If you are compelled to make a stupid joke, at least don't repeat it.

Getting cash: the problem of pricing

There is actually a whole science of *pricing theory*. (If you're really in a weird mood, but don't want to take a college course, you can have a look at *Elementary Price Theory* by Peter Dooley. It almost manages to make the subject entertaining.) I've studied this, and you don't need to: not only is pricing theory boring (unless statistics are a big passion), but the science doesn't work very well when the merchant is selling unique items in a market with both sporadic demand and near-random supply.

There's no room for science because it's pretty unlikely that you'll sell the same book more than once. If you're selling non-new items, then the chance of *any* sort of reproducibility is about zero. When our real-world shop was open, I had two copies of a book on the shelves. Between orders, it had been reprinted without changes, and not only was the new version not quite as good-looking, but the retail price had been raised.

Guess which one sold first? That's when I understood that there was little absolute logic involved in sales.

Figuring out how much you are going to charge for your item is more art than science – in fact, almost entirely art. That may feel just *wrong*; after all, we're talking about *numbers* here, the basis for *science*. The art of pricing takes a little more practice than just looking things up on a chart or running your calculator. After a few dozen listings, you'll have as good a knack for it as any Amazon.com seller can hope to have.

I won't bore you with any of the theories, but basically **the cash value of something is whatever you can get for it**. If you have a dog-chewed copy of Dean Koontz's absolutely best-selling novel, and the most common printing at that, and in a fit of whimsy you list it for $500… well, if someone pays you $500 for it, and is satisfied, then that's the value of that particular item, to that person, in that time and place.

There's a rule that every horse-trader, auctioneer, and marketplace haggler knows by heart: odds are that, if you make a sale, **you might have gotten more** for it if you'd waited for the next guy, or pushed a bit harder, or thrown in some practically worthless extra. But those professional bargainers also know the interrelated rule: **time is money**. To borrow from George Patton (who swiped from the Vikings – the Norse guys, not the football team), "A *good* plan today is better than a *perfect* plan tomorrow." You could have waited and gotten a better buck, sure… but having that extra cash in your pocket *right now* gives you the chance to take advantage of bargains that won't be there tomorrow. You give a little in order to have that extra leverage.

The variables are enormous. In the end, it comes down to your intuition as you set a number to how much you can get and how long it'll take you to get it. Rather than bore you to tears, let's look at some core thoughts about how to pare the guesswork down so that, when you finally flip a coin, you'll be deciding between good choices. A little up-front work will save you plenty of second-guessing headaches.

Data harvest

While pricing is mostly art, you will still need data, else you're doing nothing but making an uninformed guess and ought to just pick numbers out of a hat and save yourself effort. Here are a couple of tips to get you started, handy for gathering the information that will help you set a price; use some or all of them, whatever suits your style.

From Advanced search, dig for the book like any lazy buyer would. Try the author's name and a significant word from the title, or two significant words and the author's last name. Possibly only one entry will pop up, even if you know there are seven. Amazon is very nice about giving some information out quickly, so you might already be able to get an idea as to what the typical buyer is expecting to pay. If your correctly listed item is buried under a (possibly temporary) glut of common editions, you might have to shift your asking price accordingly to encourage the diligent shopper to buy. We had a good-condition trade paper that had been out of print for almost 30 years, the only edition of the book. In its proper entry, I figured it'd be good for at least $20 quickly, maybe $30 if we waited a while. When we used this search, though, we found that it was scheduled to be reprinted as a mass paper in less than two months, for $12.95. We immediately rewrote our listing, dropping the price to $15 and stressing that it was not only somewhat collectible but that the trade size was easier to hold. It sold a couple of weeks before the new edition was released.

Since sellers are so terrible at figuring which entry to list their item under, you really need to ferret out as many entries as you can and check all the Used & new listings. One title had more than a dozen entries for various editions. Half of these were long out of print and none was available used. Two were very expensive hardbounds. One, though, was a mass paper with almost 200 used copies listed, with dozens as "penny books." This was the clump with which our item would have to compete, even though ours properly belonged under a rarer entry. When I buy reading copies for myself, I'm likely to grab the nearest one-cent book that doesn't sound too mangled, and not dig through all the entries – when I just want to read, $3.50 (Amazon shipping plus one cent for the book) is not a major investment. In situations like this, you have a simple choice to make: purposely mislist your item, or trash it. We decided to stay the high road, and gave it away. Though I have a tiny bit sympathy if you choose the other path, I can't recommend it, as that merely helps muck things up further, and probably won't get you a sale anyway.

If the author is still active, take a look at her or his most recent title. A few seconds of research can tell you which editions Amazon customers are being sent to under the Customers who bought this book also bought section, and the "in addition" and "instead of" sections. If you have an uncommon edition, you might want to add your recommendation to raise your item's visibility. Again, take this into account when setting a price.

Don't bottom-feed

My company rarely lists as the cheapest item unless its condition absolutely dictates. There are a few reasons for this.

Rule 1. Our friends in the publishing industry warned us that books have an unacknowledged emotional value. Many new books being published have their prices purposely inflated by a few dollars, because the publisher's market research has found that lowering the price actually makes customers think the book is worth less. My experience with Amazon.com bears this out. Raising the price can make your item appear more valuable, if you do so intelligently.

Rule 2. As I will show you in the next chapter, lowballing your price in order to perhaps have a better chance at grabbing a sale is a loser's game. We have figured out that many Amazon Marketplace sellers have done absolutely nothing to understand what their real overhead is; while they may be making a gross profit from items they have received for free, they have shown no interest in calculating overhead costs that any real businessperson would factor in as real dollars. You must never lose track of the hard fact that, even if you get a book for free, your time spent in listing an item and processing it for shipment constitutes real value. If your trade booms, you could spend a hundred hours a month just packing books for shipment and writing labels – and if your time has no value, then you have a hobby, not a business. A dollar difference in price, accumulated over dozens of books, could spell the difference between demonstrable profit and real loss. In general, we do not list a book unless we can justify pricing it for at least $3.95 more than we paid for it. Find a similar guideline for yourself, and stick to it.

Rule 3. Under each of New, Used, and Collectible, Amazon.com shows the five cheapest listings on the initial Used & new page. The difference between the cheapest and the fifth cheapest could be substantial; in one example, the first three were one-cent books, the fourth was priced at $3.50, and the fifth $5.65. All you need to do to gain favored status on this page is have it a penny cheaper than the fifth, rather than compete for the bottom of the heap. Using this as a guide, we have occasionally *raised* our asking price to edge into that fifth slot rather than lower. Of course, we can get nudged out more easily, but we've noticed how often it is these fifth-place books that are our best sellers. Many buyers are wary of a sight-unseen bargain that simply sounds too good to be true; when you introduce a little honest disclosure, you might be satisfying this skepticism.

Rule 4. If you are selling a desirable item, dedicated shoppers will go out of their way to peruse the entire available collection of listings. Collectibles, for instance, are collectible for a wide variety of reasons, and many such listings are bogus, the descriptions valueless or nonexistent. Someone else's $12.95 listing that only says *Very good* with no further information might seem significantly more shady than your well-described $15.95 copy – you are clearly selling a real book, they're selling a pig in a poke. You may be pleasantly surprised to find that yours sells first. This can sometimes appear to be in direct conflict with Rule 3, but it's actually a matter of two different type of buyer. A few months ago, we sold a first printing of a novel that's been popular for twenty years. Priced at $47, it was about twenty-fifth under the Collectible listings, yet someone sought it out and decided that our entry was trustworthy.

Getting stuff: optimizing your inventory

Books are everywhere. During the spring, you can't walk down a residential street without seeing a sign for a garage sale or rummage sale. Estate sales are clearing out the accumulation of decades. Churches and fraternal organizations have fund-raising tag sales. Even the big chain stores need to clean out excess accumulations and damaged copies. Some of my company's best purchases have come from major grocery stores where, for reasons we cannot fathom, there was a big bin of cheap books near the cashier lanes. Keep your eyes open for opportunities, and perhaps even ask friends to alert you to caches they encounter.

Bulky surprises

If you're fortunate enough to know of a long-established used-book store, the proprietors are usually thrilled to have you walk out with a sack of their inexpensive titles; one of my suppliers says she has no interest in putting time into the Internet and would be not just satisfied but thankful if I sold her entire inventory at inflated prices, as some of them have been there for a decade, merely gathering dust and slowly moldering.

I'll let you in on a secret, gleaned from a simple bit of wisdom: **keep your ears open**. I got into the Amazon trade largely because of one "too good to be true" nugget I picked up this way. Ten years ago, I got to chatting with an owner of such a shop. Her preference was for good-quality hardcovers, but many people who wanted to sell an accumulation would bring multiple cases of books. When she rejected half, the sellers, unwilling to drag them back home, would happily pocket their profits while asking if she'd mind that they'd just as soon leave the losers there. She told me that there were two young men who would stop by weekly to sell items to her that they'd unearthed, and also happily take the castoffs away. Curious, she asked why. As it turns out, they had a regular circuit of booksellers, and would divide those castoffs into categories that each shop was interested in for their next business call. These guys were actually paying part of their college tuition from the revenues they generated. (One shopkeeper isn't kidding when she begs me to clear these away from around her door. "Sell them, give them away, burn them – I don't care, just get them out of here!" She sometimes cannot unlock the door in the morning for the boxes left on the steps my misguided but well-meaning neighbors.)

We pick up the occasional box of books for little or nothing; the term we use is *ballast,* referring to the rocks stored in the hold of a ship to keep it low in the water (and thus stable) when empty or carrying a profitable but low-mass load. If someone offers you fifty or more books for a dollar or two, someone attracted to trading used books in the first place is hopelessly hooked on the bargain.

In some of these loads, more than half is recent romances and trashy novels, so don't expect that it's all going to be gold (or even silver). Other times, you get a bunch of textbooks and technical manuals that are hopelessly out of date but not odd or old enough to be curiosities – a reference book for the Coleco Adam might find a home, but not the IBM PC-AT.

Toss out the unreadables, route the unsellables (stripped covers and the like) to people who will enjoy the reading, weed out the titles that aren't worth your while to list (these can many times get a dollar or two from your local used-book shop, and as donations might be appreciated by adult-literacy programs and community clinics for the waiting room), and the few that remain will probably compensate for your investment of money and effort.

Exercise caution, though, or you could end up with a garage full of moldy, rotten paper that in the end will only bulk up your trash. Don't encourage people (even friends) to just drop stuff on your stoop. This is one of those times where, if you must give people your business address, make it a post-office box; hand out your telephone number and e-mail address, and offer to collect their ballast books in person.

Avoid losers - and winners!

There are two specific sorts of books that we steer clear of: current hot items, and recent million-sellers. Unless you've stumbled across a particularly fine signed copy, don't even bother with most Stephen King novels, for instance – the competition is vast and the supply is glutted. (Now, if you have a mass-market first edition of, say, *The Running Man*, under the "Richard Bachman" pseudonym, then you've got a highly marketable item, because only a few thousand were ever printed, and most of those were destroyed when they didn't sell.)

The same goes for Danielle Steele, V.C. Andrews, almost all Tom Clancy, and so on. After a few decades, this could change, because today's ultra-hot author is tomorrow's forgotten curiosity. In 2003, we bought a 1960s mass paper for a dollar, *The Blood of the Lamb* by Peter de Vries, and quickly sold it for $15, because he still has a small following but is long out of print, even though he was a hot item in his day. This varies within a particular author's output, too: *The Harrad Experiment* by Robert Rimmer isn't worth listing, but just about anything else by him is worth $10 and up. The "Travis McGee" novels by John MacDonald aren't worth much, but his science fiction is scarce. Some of the best-selling books of the twentieth century have been out of print for decades. There is no way that I could tip you to a significant list of these little gems – and that's why you need to haunt Amazon.com and do your research. Your local used-book shop might have hundreds of old books that are just gathering dust; if you find homes for them, and make a nice profit in the transaction, then everyone wins.

In general, avoid acquiring best-sellers unless you have someplace to donate them to when they turn out to be unmarketable. Nobody wants to see another pristine hardcover copy of *The Celestine Prophecy* (look it up for yourself), and you'll have difficulty unloading it for even a few cents on Amazon. Titles like this will sit on your inventory shelf for years before they even have a chance at a decent price. If you inherit a few in a box, fine, but don't go out of your way to obtain them.

Targeted inventory

To have an edge, you ought to be spending at least an hour or two every week just dredging through the Amazon.com entries, looking up subjects and authors that are of interest to you as a reader or listener, and then following a few of the offered links to related books. In short, maintain a solid grasp of how the buyer – your potential customer – experiences the Amazon world.

When you spot an item that is a little scarce and selling used at a good price, write down the title. If there is the remotest chance that you are going to have a little time to stop into a bookstore, take this list along with you. When you actually do get to such a shop, also jot down the title of anything that looks interesting, and is being offered inexpensively, then look these up when you can. If a proprietor asks what I'm up to, I simply say that I'm researching an article (which I usually am) and I want to make sure I'm saving my money for only the most relevant books, so I'll have to check my notes when I get home and decide which ones I ought to buy. As this is close to promising them another sale in the near future, they leave me alone. In this respect, used bookstores near universities are great places to the shop, because they never ask in the first place.

If you have a particular field of interest, or seem to keep coming up with sellable items in one genre, then you might want to specialize a little. My company has accidentally sidled into two specialties, management theory because we simply got a lot of remaindered books on the subject, and science fiction because we have been fans for years and have a pretty good idea of values when we're out shopping. This wasn't a conscious decision, so it will likely change with time and inventory.

The scheduled relist

Every sixty days, a book that hasn't sold gets automatically delisted by Amazon.com. The listing doesn't actually go away for another 48 hours, but in the meantime it won't appear under its entry.

This protects Amazon from becoming quickly clogged with the listings left when sellers get bored and walk away, letting their accounts lapse. Your Amazon landlord makes relisting simple, though. First, they send you an e-mail for each item. When you scroll down in one of these notes, there will be a link that offers to take you to the site to run through the relisting of that item. Clicking on this opens a new browser window, running you through the sequence you used to create the listing, allowing you to edit any of the information – except, remember, for the choice between New, Used, and Collectible; if you want to change that, then you will have to let the listing end and write a new one from scratch.

As a matter of good business practice and inventory control, you ought to have someone on your staff keeping an eye for upcoming relists. I'm going to bore you for a moment and explain why. We prefer to relist books in big chunks, but sometimes other demands interfered with the original entering, so only one or two books actually went live in that day. The result is that, sixty days later, we have to relist one or two books. Though it only takes a minute to relist without making changes, this *feels* inefficient to us. By looking ahead, we can see that maybe twenty books are going to demand attention the next day. So, we wait, sometimes stretching that 48 hours to the limit and entering the older items even as we are receiving the newer notifications. Don't wait too long, though, or Amazon will delete your listing and you'll have to start anew. But if you can move a clump one day closer to joining a bigger mass, you've at least gained yourself a bigger span where you don't have to be concerned. We scan our "open Marketplace listings" page every week or two to check up on our books. Click the **Account** button (top-right on almost any page), and on the next page (off to the right) in the box Auctions, zShops, and Marketplace, click **Your seller account**. The first bullet-point under Your Inventory is View Items; you want the one under Amazon.com Marketplace called **open**. This will bring you to a list of everything that can be purchased from you in the Marketplace, but there's one more step that'll make it useful. Off on the right is the Sort by box; select **Start Date: Old to New**, then click on **GO!** and you'll see the stuff you have that will need to be relisted first (assuming it doesn't sell before its time runs out).

Having steered you through the "official" way of doing things, I'm now going to show you how to make the tool a little more useful for you. Begin by looking for an item that you have listed – you want the actual "Used & new" listing, just like a customer would see. Once there, click on your company name, which will bring you to your main Feedback page. Under

Related Links, click **View this seller's zShop and Auctions Member Profile**. At your Member Profile page, scan down to the link **View Open Marketplace Listings** and click on it. Do you see the difference? This version of your inventory listing displays something very handy: the exact moment that item will require relisting, down to the second. When you display them old-to-new, you will immediately know how they cluster and, unless you take a vacation, you can mark on your calendar when the next bunch needs to be relisted.

The scheduled relist is simple and (usually) fast. When an item is marked for expiration, Amazon sends an e-mail to your account – easy to recognize for the words "listing has expired" at the end of the subject line. When you get this note, should you try to do a normal search, you won't be able to see your listing. So, scroll down a screen in the e-mail, past the brief item description and the line If you would like to relist this item now, follow this link where you'll see a long and complicated Web address. Click this, and a new browser window will open. Here, you can change every part of your listing except the category, or scan the other listings to see if its value or availability has changed since you last listed. When you are satisfied with the listing, go to the orange **Preview your changes** button at the bottom of the info. The system then shows you what will be contained in the listing – if you're satisfied, click the **Submit** button.

Even on a slow Internet connection, it usually take less than a minute to relist an item, from opening the e-mail to the final Your listing is now live! screen.

The one quibble I have is that you have to relist your books one after the other. If you try to do it with two books at the same time, Amazon will almost always send both sets of requests to the same browser window, possibly losing the information on the previous screen. I remind myself constantly that it only adds another minute or two to a long stack of relistings, and not to get impatient with a pretty efficient process.

When we go into the relist process, we try to group them, just for the sake of neatness. For instance, we'll do all the science fiction, then the rest of the fiction, then all business books, then the New Age stuff, and so on. This lines up the relisting a little better with our physical shelving arrangements – simply a bit of organization.

There is one more thing you might want to do to streamline the process a little. After months of selling on Amazon, I finally had a stroke of intelligence. I went into the e-mail software on our computer (we use Outlook Express, but every other package I've seen has something similar) and told it to route all messages from Amazon.com into a new folder called "Book Business." (One of these days, we will route the orders, the relist notices, and the notices of deposit to separate subfolders.) If you do something like this, you greatly cut down on the chances that a big sale will get lost in the spam – or, worse, thrown out accidentally.

The forced relist

For all sorts of reason, you might want to yank a particular item out of your Amazon listings. You may have sold the book elsewhere, or decided to give it away as a gift or add it to your personal collection. Maybe you're having doubts about the price, or its collectability has shot up – or plummeted, if a long-overdue new edition has finally become available.

There are two general reasons for spontaneously messing with your listing, though:

- you are no longer selling it on Amazon.com, or
- you need to make changes.

Luckily, both operations are fast and easy.

To kill the listing, go to the "official" listing of your items (via the "Your seller account" page, as described above) and click on the **Edit or close this listing** button for the item you want to kill or modify. This will take you to a screen almost identical to that used to relist items, with the significant addition of a **Close this listing now** button near the top. (If you want to close the listing, Amazon will ask you for your reason. While they might deserve a simple explanation, we can't see any good reason to go into great detail.)

So far, we've only had to do one forced delisting. A book had been entered as merely used, and I happened to notice it on the shelf and spot it for collectible. Since there were so few available, I didn't see any reason to change the category, but the price was far too low. I killed the listing until we could figure out how to price it, rather than risk having it sell before we could raise the price appropriately. For our official reason, we simply wrote "put under wrong entry," and nobody questioned it.

In hindsight, if I had been prepared to make a pricing decision on the spot, I would have simply edited the listing.

A little more edge

Since we're looking at the relisting process, let me give you another boost: Keep an eye on your books to make sure they're not drastically changing value while you sleep. Really, you *ought* to do this every few weeks, but there are only so many hours in a day, and that's a lot of busywork once your inventory starts numbering in the hundreds. The scheduled relist gives you a perfect opportunity to do this, and acts as an automatic reminder service.

I tweak prices mercilessly, though generally only at scheduled relist. In the sixty days since an item was listed, there is the possibility that the market for that title has changed substantially. Maybe I had one of three listed copies of a long-unavailable book, and now it's back in print; I ought to chop the price to stay competitive. A few times, we put the item up when there was a bit of a selection, then found that almost all of them had disappeared, increasing the value of ours. There is sometimes a run primarily on the more-expensive or the less-expensive items; once in a while, the middle falls out of the market, and you may want to trim your price to fit into either the high-end or low-end camp.

Every once in a while, you will list a moderately priced item. Weeks or months later, you'll happen to take a look at the other available copies, and one of the strange literary trends will have swept through that's resulted in almost all the lower-priced listings disappearing. At this point, you'll have to stop and wonder whether it's prudent to raise the price (maybe by a substantial amount) and possibly miss the trend, or leave it pretty much where it is and get that item out of your inventory and converted into proper cash.

Of course, things go the other way as well. You might have made the first listing while your item was the only one presently available on Amazon. Since then, a dozen more have appeared, all with a lower price and some of them sounding substantially nicer. Again, you can drop the price and catch a possible sales trend, or you hold to the price and wait until those other items are scooped up, clearing the field.

Lest you think there's any science involved with this: no. I can't even call it art – it's all intuition and educated guesswork. Follow your hunches, whether to leave it alone or change it.

How the numbers actually work

I've worked in the computer, customer service, and data collection fields for most of my life. So far, I've spotted at least a half-dozen really interesting pieces of software as part of Amazon.com's infrastructure. I couldn't tell you which impresses me more: the utility of the data that is returned; the lack of intrusiveness; the ways customers are encouraged to participate and become part of a community.

But, by far, the most impressive feature of this software is that, even if you happen to be a serious power-shopper on the site, you've probably never consciously noticed any of this fancy programming.

With that said, some of the data that goes flying past in transactions isn't even that obvious. If you are going to be a successful seller, you need to at least know some details of the mechanism you are using. I'm going to take a moment to reveal some details of the Amazon.com cash flow that very few sellers even consider, much less understand.

Shaving nickels to serve you better

When a customer buys an item on Amazon from a Marketplace listing, there is a shipping charge levied, which is then passed along to the seller as a credit for shipping costs. This is very nice. What most people don't notice is that Amazon takes a cut. They shave points on the sale, they shave points on the postage.

If you don't like any of this, don't even get started, just leave quietly. It ain't gonna change! And why should it – it's working, everyone involved derives value, and Amazon.com owns the ball, the court, the referees, and the copyrights to the rulebook. You can follow the rules as they've dictated them, or you can probably dig up another game somewhere else.

I'm hardly complaining. This is a great business model, and satisfied players vastly outnumber anyone who might be griping. Once I ran the numbers, I started thinking about how to maximize my company's percentage.

A typical sale

Let's take a look at this. My company shipped a book recently.

We listed it at	\$4.99
When it sold, Amazon also collected for shipping	\$3.49
The customer thus paid	\$8.48
Amazon collected their cut, 15% of price plus 99¢	\$1.74
Our account was credited with	\$3.25
As the customer selected Standard shipping, we were also credited for	\$2.26
Amazon received the remaining	\$1.23
From this sale, Amazon made	\$2.97
We got a total of	\$5.51

Postage cost us \$1.86, for a gross profit of \$3.65. Factor in the cost of listing the book, processing the sale, packing the order, and standing in line at the post office – call it 15 minutes total, at \$10.00 per hour, or \$2.50. In the end, we got \$1.15… less costs of packaging, and the book itself.

This is why it is very important that you have a streamlined operation, and that you get your merchandise for as little as possible.

How we screwed up

A while back, we had a minor internal fiasco that taught us some valuable lessons. I'm going to repeat the above with a few changes.

We listed a book at	\$12.50
Amazon collected shipping of	\$3.49
The customer paid	\$15.99
Amazon got 15% of price plus 99¢	\$2.87
Our account was credited with	\$9.63
With Standard shipping, we were credited for	\$2.26
Amazon received the remaining	\$1.23

From this sale, Amazon made	$4.10
We got a total of	$11.89

This looks really good. Problem is, it was a big hardcover, for which we'd paid about $4.35. Because it was a pain to pack, total processing time was almost half an hour, or a value of $5.00, and postage was almost $4.00. For all that hassle, then, we netted less than three bucks.

We learned to avoid big and heavy items unless we could mark the price up accordingly.

The mystery of the penny books

Something we still can't figure out is the many dealers who look at an unremarkable item, and decide to take on the inevitable. Often, there are a few hundred of this title listed, mostly in excellent condition. My company has a policy that such items are given away as gifts, donated to various organizations, or (if they're in truly poor shape) quietly dropped in the trash.

Other folks, though, list them anyway, and they glut the bottom of the listings as one-cent books. The transaction looks something like this.

They offer the book at	$0.01
Amazon collects shipping of	$3.49
The customer pays	$3.50
Amazon's cut, 15% of price plus 99¢, is	$0.99
The seller's account apparently gets	-$0.98
With Standard shipping, they also get	$2.26
Amazon gets	$1.23
Amazon makes a total of	$2.22
The seller must receive	$1.28

Even if packed in stolen envelopes by slave labor, that sale loses money because postage alone is probably going to be more than a dollar. It loses even more if they paid *anything* for the book, or it's a hardbound (thus more expensive to ship). The choice is yours, but I'd advise against it.

Okay, there's a gimmick that partially explains many of the "penny book" listings. As I'll discuss at the end of the book, those merchants who sign up for the Pro Merchant program ($39.99/month) pay a significantly smaller commission to

Amazon. You can see how, especially for low-end books, this can allow for competition that a basic-level merchant can't touch without losing money on the deal.

Even then, I don't see where this sort of item is worth even having on the shelves. You could sell it at your next garage sale for maybe a quarter, and save yourself effort. But, to each his own.

A good score

Here's one more example, after which you can do your own math. We had a slim trade paperback that a little research showed was unusual, if not rare. It cost us $2.20, and we quickly sold it to a British customer.

We listed it at	45.00
Amazon charged shipping of	$9.79
The customer paid	$54.79
Amazon took 15% plus 99¢, or	$7.74
We received	$37.26
For shipping, we got a further	$8.95
Amazon kept	$0.84
Amazon's total take was	$8.58
Ours was	$46.21

Packaging wasn't any more onerous a chore than typically, and since airmail postage happened to be only $8.46, we further pleased a customer.

We've had bigger profits, but this has formed a sort of target for us. A dozen such sales per month, and our business chugs merrily along.

Realistic income expectations

In books such as you are reading, authors are practically expected to make ridiculous promises, stuff you shouldn't even believe in your wildest dreams, like "Get rich without getting off your sofa!" or "Support your family without ever working again!"

Well, I'm not one of them. By following what I tell you here, and picking up some vital skills, and keeping your eyes open, you can hope to set up a nice little sideline or augment your real-world trade in books and CDs and other stuff. With some diligence and a lot of luck, sure, you can improve on this. Someday, you may even have both a steady on-line income and a nice little shop that more than pays its way. With that in mind, I want to go over some of the numbers and hard facts with you, in hope that you might be able to tweak the realities for your particular situation.

Let's say that you want to make the equivalent of a good basic job from your venture into the Marketplace. Ten bucks an hour in a full-time job isn't enough to retire on, but it's not terrible, especially since you'll be able to work flexible hours from just about anywhere in the known Universe (as long as it has dialup access to the Internet, at least). For the sake of illustration, let's call that income level $400 a week, or $1,600 per month, coming out to something like an annual gross of $20,000. If this is your primary source of income, you'd have to account for various taxes, but I'll ignore that here.

Our experience has been that we sell one book per week for every 100 we have listed on the Marketplace. That's hardly scientific, but seems to be vaguely accurate.

Assume that each and every item you sell brings you an even $5.00 after costs of acquisition, listing, storage, picking, and shipping.

When you put all this together, you would have to sell an average of 80 items per week to have that steady income.

If our experience holds true, you would have to maintain an inventory of 8,000 listed items to have this sort of volume. Since a single head-high bookshelf holds roughly 500 items, that means that some part of your home or office is going to have room for at least eight extra-deep shelving units, with access to both sides. (If you are already maintaining a shop, of course, you're off the hook in this respect.)

Your cost in time doesn't look so bad, though. Once you get the hang of it, each item you sell will have taken you as little as 15 minutes for everything from the initial listing on Amazon.com to waiting in line at the post office. Those 80 items therefore set you back all of 20 hours a week. In short, your gross income is something like $20 an hour, which is not a bad return at all.

Can you get rich? It's possible, if you can manage to come up with a regular flow of unusual items that have a high demand. After all, if you sell at the same rate as I've outlined, but your profit per item is more like $20, you can either pocket a more generous cash return, or make a nice steady income working only a few hours a week – to make the $400 target, you'd give up a mere five hours.

All in all, getting rich is not a reason to start into this sort of business, and having that as a main goal might undercut good business decision-making. However, if you love books and music, and would like to make a few extra dollars along the way, you could find this to be a personally rewarding venture. And that's as much of a promise as I am going to make.

Book business basics on Amazon.com, part I: tracking your traffic

Much of this chapter is going to stem from the assumption that you don't have a whole lot of experience with selling books, selling online, or even running your own small business. On the other hand, I've helped more than a few established businesses in my career, and found some glaring omissions that resulted in a whole lot of headache, heartbreak, cash loss, or legal hassles. Whatever your degree of experience, give this chapter at least one thorough reading. And if you are indeed one of those good folks for whom this is a new venture, I hope you'll come back and re-read it occasionally.

Your main "slip" system

Besides my love of books, my biggest contribution to our little company is a bit of talent at setting up tracking systems for small businesses.

Everyone who jumps into the Marketplace ought to have something like our primary system of tracking slips. First, of course, are the slips themselves. These are easy to produce if you have access to a computer, or a typewriter, or even just a photocopier. Ours are very simple, with lines for:

- acquisition date
- price paid
- Amazon entry date
- listed price

When an item sells, we use the back of its slip to note the title, the date of sale, and any changes in price since the initial listing.

Creating slips is no big thing. You can use a label template in your word processor software if you want it as fast and easy as possible. I like to have "cut here" lines, though, so I just define a table that fills the entire page, format it to have lines between all the cells, create one slip I'm happy with, then copy this to all the cells. The fancier you get, the more you'll have to tweak – once it's done, though, save the file and pull it up when you need more slips.

I would discourage you from getting too complex in the amount of data you track on each book. If you've only got one or two hundred books, more information won't help you, and just adds to clutter. If you've got one or two thousand, you need a more automated system anyway. Nevertheless, you may wish to add spaces on your slips to track:

- where you got it from
- what category it's listed in (New or Used, Very Good or Acceptable)
- what rank it has in that category (for tracking of supply and demand)
- whether you feel like the price you set might be too high or low
- how much you'll receive when it sells (minus the Amazon fee)
- what your shipping credits will be

This is only the "front end" of our system. After we make a sale and hand our shipments for the day off to the Post Office, the slips are clipped to the USPS receipt, as well as related receipts if any special packaging was required.

I set up a simple spreadsheet on my PC to track our sales. I'm admittedly too lazy to do this for our entire inventory, but there's no reason for you not to track all your items if that's your inclination. Our spreadsheet has columns for:

- title
- author/artist
- date purchased
- price paid
- source
- date entered on Marketplace
- date sold
- price received
- shipping method
- cost of shipping

Don't let any of this intimidate you. My father still does most of his business tracking on sheets of meticulously hand-lined typing paper, because he enjoys making these forms after a hard day. You might want to do something like that, or print them out from a spreadsheet program, or set it up as a table in a word-processor, or simply buy standard ledger pages at an office-supply store. Whatever works best for you is, by definition, the best system.

Further tracking: optional but useful

Our two secondary systems are in place to help us track troublesome items.

More often than we like, we find that a particular item doesn't appear anywhere on Amazon.com, or at least not in any obvious way. The book may have been entered under a variant title without the author's name, for example.

Generally, though, that book simply ain't there. We therefore made up a sheet of small slips that each say **This title not listed on Amazon.com as of __________.** We write the date on the slip and insert it into the book, then it goes into a box with the rest. Every few months, we pull the box and check again, because old books regularly reappear in print. This also gives us the opportunity to consider whether it's worth putting out at all and often a book will end up in our give-away box. If it's particularly collectible-looking, though, we might decide that we'd be better off selling it to an actual bookstore for a few dollars. Once in a while, we find that book has been listed, but under a different title, and sometimes a mistake was made in the entry that has been corrected.

My bibliophilia is in some ways a bad addiction. At any given moment, I have dozens of books sitting on my "to be read" shelf. Instead of using up my limited memory, I made up another slip that reads **Not worth listing on Amazon as of __________.** That way, I don't waste too much time checking the same book month after month.

These are only suggestions, of course. As you develop a business style of your own, you may find that the minutes you spend making up tracking slips can save you hours of work every month. It's not as if there is any significant investment involved so if you change your mind after a few weeks, you can modify your system or drop it entirely. Remember: the primary purpose should be that the time you spend on business-related matters is adding to your profits, and eliminating necessary but unpaid tasks must always be important if you are going to maximize your success.

Dealing with customers

If a buyer (or potential buyer) asks you a question, then for heaven's sake *answer it promptly*. Be friendly, not defensive. Thank them for their order or their interest. When I talk to other sellers, Internet and real-world, some of them react to this as if I were asking them to knock out a few of their own teeth with a hammer. This sort of contact costs you nothing but a few minutes of your precious time. If you're not a naturally friendly person, then at least try to fake it.

Lost orders

I do have to admit to my own slight dishonesty. It's not something that I am proud of, even though it worked out fine for everyone. A book we sent disappeared in the mail system for six weeks, and the buyer contacted us. I immediately sent her a note apologizing for the delay (even though there was nothing we could do about it), and pulled the USPS receipt out of the file. I told her the exact minute it had been shipped, and promised to look into it, which is essentially impossible for a media-mail item, promising a speedy refund if nothing could be done. Two days later, she sent us another note to say that it had arrived and thanking us for our diligence. Basically, I fudged the truth and stalled. Be *very* careful about doing this – you are playing with fire – and be prepared to issue that refund.

Even if your company is spotlessly diligent about filling orders, there are still many hands through which it must pass. If you are mailing an item from somewhere to somewhere else within the continental United States, then 99% of what you ship (if it's smaller than a major appliance and weighs less than half a ton) will arrive within six weeks, no matter what shipping method is used. If you send an item that disappears for that long, then you ought to give up, assume it's entirely lost, and submit a refund. The only exception would be if you find that Amazon shipments to that customer appear to go astray with regularity – that's one of the reasons that merchants really ought to be diligent about leaving feedback about their customers. If you're selling an item for a few dollars, fraud probably isn't involved... and if someone is willing to work that hard to rip you off for a few dollars, then you'd be happier giving in to their demands and hoping you never encounter them again.

Refunds

In short, prompt refunds are a good thing.

Basically, if you can't complete a sale within eight weeks, you should give back the money. Sometimes, it simply gets lost in transit. If you have a real-world store, and you sell an item on Amazon that has already been sold, then don't substitute and don't look for a replacement so you can fill the order – inform the customer that you're setting up a refund, and let that customer decide whether they'd like to try again.

This is good public relations in any case. When I first became an Amazon customer, the second book I ever ordered disappeared utterly. I think it was all of four dollars, but I did want to read that book, so I dropped a note to the seller asking if it had been sent, and how long they thought I ought to wait before applying for a refund. Bless them, they said that it had been a full eight weeks in transit and was probably dead, so they would just submit a refund request. Three days later, the book arrived in the mail. I sent another note, thanking them for their responsiveness, and for the book, offering to arrange payment. They thanked me for my honesty, and told me to enjoy the book. Really, it eats into profits at every contact, so they were wisely cutting their losses at that point – but I admit to feeling a tiny bit better about them, and will choose to buy from them again if presented with similar items.

Speaking as a seller, whether or not the item ever arrives, I would rather have a pleased (okay, less-irritated) customer, and write off the loss as a cost of doing business or as a marketing expense. Unhappy customers tend to be more vocal than the happy ones, and word might spread quickly that you come across as an unresponsive jerk who scrabbles after every penny. It's unlikely that you will ever have to issue a refund for even one item in a thousand, so consider it a great opportunity to keep your business reputation polished.

We'll go into the mechanics of refunds in the next chapter.

Profit/loss

Furthermore, when writing off that refund, I would include the value of the time spent entering the lost item in the first place, and of preparing it for shipment, and of communication with the buyer. I can justify that the time to my company is reasonably worth $10 per hour, and our accountant deals with it appropriately.

That's something that I can't emphasize enough: this is a *business*. Your time has value. You need to track everything, and to figure that into your balance sheet, otherwise you are really going to have no idea as to whether you are making or losing money on this venture. In your tracking system – the slips and the spreadsheet – you might want to note if a particular item was particularly troublesome. If you had to drive ten miles and search for a half-hour through an office-supply store to get a suitable box, then you have every right to charge for that time against the profits your business makes.

When in doubt, sit down for a chat with an accountant or bookkeeper. There are many of these about who specialize in businesses who only need their services for a few hours a month, and they can probably save you more than you pay them by intelligent record-keeping and tax preparation.

Taxes?

Yes, you owe taxes. If you don't make much, then the odds of the Internal Revenue Service or your state's sales-tax office coming after you are pretty much nonexistent. Still, should you start to make a good flow of cash, then your visibility as a target begins to increase, and they might have some questions about the revenue history of your enterprise – and your life will be a lot happier if you are ready with honest and thorough answers, and that includes proof that you've been paying what you owe all along.

What you really need is a bookkeeper who will guide you through all this. Usually, the accounting process is easy enough to do yourself, but sometimes a professional can readily steer you to lower tax risk and higher profitability. Whole books are written about these subjects, but I want to make a couple of comments on important points.

In most states, you are required to collect sales tax for

items you sell to your fellow residents, and to send these taxes to the appropriate office on a certain schedule. One option is to simply not sell to buyers from your state – really, though, this somewhat defeats the purpose of going into business in the first place, and limits your opportunities for self-marketing to people you know. If you don't already have a sales-tax number, contact your state's bureau of taxation and revenue, who likely can also steer you toward collecting any city or county sales taxes that you need to deal with.

Another reason to have this number is that it allows you to buy stuff without paying sales tax, as long as that stuff is purchased specifically to resell it (presumably, therefore, collecting sales tax on a higher price). Some areas require that you leave a *non-taxable purchase certificate* (or similar wording) on file with whoever you're buying from, so that they can explain the resultant discrepancies to the tax authorities. Others require you to pay the sales tax on your purchases, but allow you to present your receipts to deduct almost all of the sales tax from revenues you owe. Again, this depends on where you're living, so you'll have to ask your local bureaucracies for exact information.

Technically, most states also require a *compensating* or *use* tax to be collected for items bought in another state for personal use. The theory behind this is that it levels the playing field, so that residents aren't going across the border to save a few bucks, and thus depriving local merchants of trade. In reality, these are awfully hard to track without adding a whole new bureaucratic tax-collecting office and fighting off "restraint of trade" challenges in the courts. Nevertheless, there has been discussion for years about states ganging together to form "compacts" where they will collect each other's taxes; fortunately, the implementation is enough of a nightmare that this may never come to pass. At this point, my feeling is that Amazon will let us know if these plans affect the mechanics of selling on their site.

As a rule of thumb, a business has some tax privileges, but the IRS doesn't want people to be using perpetual "business losses" as a way of hiding personal income, so there are a few things they are going to expect from you to maintain your business status. At the top of the list is that your business is allowed to take a loss in two years out of a consecutive five without Internal Revenue giving you too hard a time. (Those loss years don't have to be consecutive.) Should you do it more often, or make big claims, you'll increase the likelihood that you're raising big red flags as well. That three-in-five profitability, even then, is a guideline: you have more leeway if you can demonstrate that you are operating in a clearly businesslike manner, and not just as a hobby.

If your Marketplace efforts start making big bucks, then find yourself a good accountant who can help you with businesslike ways of putting your cash to use in ways other than paying taxes. If you should happen to show an embarrassing profit, then the end of the year is a good time to add to inventory or upgrade your equipment; again, don't spend so much that you're taking a loss, but instead reducing the amount of taxable profit. At some point, you might even like to be paid for your work; there are ways to do this without causing yourself undue tax problems either personally or in your company. And be sure to talk to your specialist about deducting the space and equipment that you use for your Amazon venture.

A comment from our bookkeeper: Maintain separate bank accounts for your business ventures and for your personal use – and keep them scrupulously separate. Using your personal account to pay company bills is sloppy; using your company funds to pay your personal bills gets the wrong sort of attention, especially if you're trying to claim business-related expenses as deductible. If you're fortunate, you'll only have your deductions denied.

All in all, don't start out assuming that your company is so small that it has no tax consequences. That's sloppy thinking, and will only lead to trouble. You may well have no tax consequences… but do the paperwork before you believe it.

Book business basics on Amazon.com, part II: closing the sale

At this point, you have a merchant account on Amazon.com, you have physical inventory, and it's properly listed for the whole Internet world to peruse. Now comes the fun part.

The Arrival

That's when the fateful e-mail tells you that an item has sold. Once in a while, there will be another note sent immediately before it informing you that the buyer has yet to provide complete and up-to-date information for their purchase. If you receive these in the wrong order – it happened to us once – you may think that the order has been canceled. Read carefully!

The notification contains all sorts of information. Some of the data fields apply only to Amazon Advantage sellers, and I won't consider those here. Most of the rest, though, help you complete the sale, and can also make you appear more professional.

Touch base

As soon as you get the e-mail, go to your physical inventory and pull that item off the shelf. It's not unusual that we have five or six copies of a particular title on our shelves, though, all at different prices depending on condition. If you have similar doubts about an order, scroll down that e-mail past the PACKING SLIP portion, and on a line beginning Listing 1 you'll see a link. Click this and you'll be taken to your description for that exact item.

Then, reassured that you can actually keep up your end of the bargain, scroll down to the end of the information in that e-mail and send off a note to the buyer, telling them that it's about to be sent, what day it's likely to be shipped, and thanking them for the purchase.

Again, I'm lazy, so I created a system that uses someone else's work to make us look more professional. We copy the data area from Amazon's note, then paste it into our outgoing message. We quickly delete lines that we don't use (like the PLU number) and our e-mail address that Amazon sent to since we use a different out-bound address for customer contact.

Sending a simple note such as this off to your customer is a nice personal touch that lets them feel more connected to you as an individual merchant, rather than as an order-filler for Amazon. This also gives the buyer a chance to ask that we send the item elsewhere, or to otherwise correct the ship-to address. As a final bit of edge, we ask them to let us know if there are any problems, and to post feedback at Amazon when the item arrives. Call it superstition, but we think this has resulted in a better response rate for feedback (see below) and for more positive comments at that. We do get a few pleasant e-mails thanking us when their order arrives.

Track the sale

The tracking slip that you put with every item in inventory can serve more purposes. When we sell an item, we make a note on the back about what it is, what date it sold, and what the actual price was. These slips are later stapled to the USPS or FedEx receipt for entry into our master spreadsheet.

Make the packing slip

As with the contact e-mail, we make up a simple packing slip using the Amazon notification. If your company is set up more along a warehouse model, you could turn this into a "pick and pack" sheet where the people actually pulling items from the shelves and preparing them for shipping can check off the items as they're found and packaged.

Don't overload your customer, but this is another great contact point. You could feature your store's address or website URL. You could print a coupon good for a discount or freebie. If you have other items in your inventory of a similar nature (they don't have to be listed on Amazon), maybe you want to offer them here. You could even put in some simple graphics to lighten it up a little bit – don't steal copyrighted material, of course, because word might get around that you're a bit less than honest. At the moment, all we use is our company logo and another short "thank you," but that could always change.

Though it isn't worth the trouble for our business, some sellers print up a sheet at this point that also bears the mailing label. We won't discuss that here, but there is software on the market that can "harvest" the data automatically and create these unitized sheets for you at the click of a mouse. Personally, I'd say that the cost of this won't come back to you unless you have thousands of items listed and are selling at least a hundred a month, so don't get too fascinated with the idea until it makes clear economic sense.

Pack it

There are many, many ways of packing books and CDs. As a rule of thumb, your packages ought to look professional and be reasonably solid. Everything after that is up to you, though I'd caution you not to go overboard, especially if you deal primarily in fairly common items.

Some sellers prefer boxes and cardboard "flat mailers" that fold securely around the item. These have the advantage of discouraging postal workers from folding an item to fit into a small mailbox. My company cannot justify the expense (and the extra shelf space) of keeping a stock of even the most common sizes, but your circumstances may be different. The best supplier we have found for a wide variety of boxes is ULINE Shipping Supplies (*www.uline.com*), with KHL Express (*www.khlexpress.com*) coming in a close second – these aren't your only choices, of course, just our favorites. An added advantage of a corrugated box or mailer is that the folded edges further stiffen the package and help protect the item.

In most cases, we use Kraft-paper envelopes with integrated bubble-wrap material. Our primary supplier of these is The Linton Company (*www. bubblemailers.biz*). As they claim on their website, they really are extraordinarily pleasant and helpful people, and they really do deliver quickly; the only drawback is that you can only order full cases online, and have to actually call them on the telephone if you want partial lots. The best prices are in buying a whole case anyway, which also results in free shipping, so I suggest spending the extra few dollars up front. As an added incentive, they use more recycled material in their products than any other supplier we've found – their Ecobubble mailers are high-quality, whether you care about environmentally friendly packaging or not. In general, when using envelopes, it's still a good idea to seal the flap edges with clear packing tape, making it less likely to get snagged and torn during shipping.

Though I think that Tyvek envelopes are a fantastic invention, some of them are so slick that postal labels don't adhere at all well, and they're impossible to write on. Usually, you'll need to add bubble-pack wrapping or other padding yourself, which adds to the cost in terms of both materials and your time in filling the order.

For expensive items, we prefer to stiffen the package further by wrapping the item in a layer of corrugated cardboard. Again, this helps to protect the item from folding or crushing in transit. A little extra wrapping is rarely a bad thing. I have been so gratified, as a customer, to receive a package that looks as though it's been run over by a forklift then attacked by rabid weasels, only to cut away the layers of mangled packaging and find that the item didn't have a single mark on it.

Unless you are sending a particularly hard-to-pack item and don't want to delay shipment while finding an alternative, I recommend that you don't recycle a used box or envelope. You can save maybe a dollar or two, but it's generally a false economy and only makes your little company look like a corporate cheapskate.

Label it

The two bits of information that are essential are the customer's shipping address and your business address. Sometimes shipping goes horribly awry, and having your address improves the odds that the thing won't get entirely lost in the system.

At first, we used a "unitized" label, a big square thing four inches on a side, with our company logo and address across the top. The Post Office diligently sent the item to us. After the third time, we gave up the fight and changed to a two-label system, so that we could separate the two addresses as much as possible on the package.

We print our own labels, using standard word-processor software. Programs such as Word have handy templates for these, and make it a snap to design one label and get a whole sheet of them. If you don't have this option, then you'll have to sacrifice an hour laying out a table that has the same dimensions as your label sheet, then copying the label to each cell – it's a bit of work, but vastly cheaper than having them professionally printed. If you have the option, though, print your labels on a laser printer, not on an inkjet; if you only have an inkjet, then cover the label with clear packing tape, or the printing will smear (even wash off) when it gets damp.

Don't go to graphic excess here! You need your label information to be quickly read and comprehended, and that means simple fonts and clean backgrounds. Though it may seem boring, it's hard to go wrong with white labels and plain black ink.

Our "upper left" label is simple but visually effective. Our company logo is on the left, and the rest of the area to the right of this is filled with our return address. We use a common 1″ by 2.5″ label sheet for this.

The main address label is 2″ by 4″ and horizontal ("the long way" rather than "the tall way" – or, if you prefer, "landscape" instead of "portrait"). We found that printing out individual labels for each shipment was slowing us down significantly, so we print up a few sheets with our logo off to the right and our company name along the bottom, then hand-write the shipping address using a fine-line permanent marker (usually a black Sharpie). If it suits your situation, printing each label might be better for you.

As a final fillip (and one recommended by Amazon), you might write on the envelope or add to one of your labels, **Here's your order from Amazon.com!** If you want to put a few initial minutes into it, you could print a sheet of these separately, in colors that suit you and your business.

Ship it

The USPS provides you with the option of printing the postage directly at your computer, whether onto a standard label or using one of the many Pitney-Bowes products. You then attach the postage and put the package out for pickup by your route carrier.

We tried this, briefly. We appear to be at the end of the carrier route, so the visit comes between noon and 6 p.m. – usually. I discovered that, if we put the package out after the mail carrier had been there, the postage will have expired by the next day, since it bore a date-stamp. Maybe you're more efficient than us, and this would be a nice option, but we've returned to the old-fashioned way and now bring our packages into the postal station.

Generally, you can get away with sending your item as "media mail," which costs less than parcel post and isn't significantly slower than any other method (with the possible exception of express).

Due to the quirks of the postal system, it is sometimes no more expensive, even cheaper, to send the item by parcel post, or even first-class or airmail. We shipped a somewhat expensive item to London, and it cost less than a dollar extra to get it there in a few days rather than up to a month. This isn't confined to overseas delivery: one package going to the next state was actually cheaper to send by the faster method. Unless you're in a big hurry, ask the person at the counter if there would be much of a difference in price.

You need to decide at what point you will purchase extra services for a shipment. For instance, insuring a $4.50 item likely doesn't make much sense, but is necessary for a $100 item, and you probably want to consider a delivery receipt, too. If you specialize in high-end items, possibly of a particular author or genre, you might want to establish a parallel high-end operation, from carefully wrapping your items and nestling them in packing-filled boxes, to splurging on all the extras the shipping agency has to offer – and, of course, setting your prices accordingly.

Solicit feedback

After you send an item off, you have another opportunity to touch base with the customer. Send an e-mail telling them when the item was shipped (including any tracking number that you may have obtained, along with a link to instructions on its use). Mention approximately when delivery should be (if you have a solid estimate), perhaps offer them any similar items you might have, and steer them to your website if you have one.

Finally, ask them to inspect the item when it arrives and enter feedback at the Amazon.com site, perhaps including a link to the proper page. We don't hesitate to remind customers that **We are a small business, and your opinion of your buying experience is very important to us!** One way or another, help your customers (in a non-pushy manner, of course) to help you. Have them click their own **Account** button, then choose **Open and recently shipped orders** in the Where's My Stuff? section. When your customer scrolls down to your transaction and clicks its **View order** button, under the shipment description section there's a Feedback area. If you're a better programmer than me, you could come up with an HTML button you can put into an e-mail note.

You might want to (gently) suggest that, if everything went smoothly, a 5 of 5 rating is appropriate, and that if they feel the transaction deserves less, you would appreciate an opportunity to discuss the problems first. I've noted that some customers give 4 of 5 without indicating a reason for their displeasure – some sellers report getting far less because a customer decided they didn't like the *author's* abilities!

I buy stuff for myself through Amazon. Sporadically, I receive a very nice e-mail message after I make a purchase, with a button that takes me directly to the feedback area for that item. Though I've asked around, I have yet to receive an answer as to what triggers this. With any luck, by the time you read this, it will be a regular feature for Marketplace merchants.

I will be honest, and tell you that the whole Feedback system is sheer voodoo. It's based on slippery assumptions, and is sporadically policed by Amazon.com. For instance:

- many honest Marketplace merchants grit their teeth and accept a rating of 4.9 or even 4.8, and go into a panic when they slump to 4.5
- a few dishonest sellers operate below 4.0, run their ratings into the ground, and, after Amazon shuts them down, shift their listings over to another Merchant account
- some customers will give you a 4 of 5 for an order about which they have no complaints, or a 2 because the plot of the movie didn't live

up to their expectations

- some shady sellers maintain multiple customer accounts, purchase their own one-cent items, and leave themselves 5 stars and sparkling comments to boost their numbers
- some of these are exceptional weasels, and have found ways to leave themselves "customer" feedback without even pretending to make a purchase

Obviously, you ought to avoid being a jerk. Sure, you can fish for naïve customers, but there are some of us who balance your price against your Feedback, and also give a little preference to sellers who have done well for us in the past.

Should Amazon someday decide to raise the bar, you could find yourself on the wrong side of the divide, maybe permanently. Explicitly banning certain practices, or even enforcing current standards, could take a big bite out of Amazon's overall customer-satisfaction problems. Not that they're worried about image: following up on complaints about the Marketplace requires human effort, which costs hard dollars. Amazon didn't get where it is by being irresponsible with cash, so they might decide to stamp out something that's bad for their business.

The dreaded refund

If things should go awry, you will be obligated to submit for a refund. Actually, it's not at all difficult.

- Go to your Seller Account page, and under "Your Transactions" click on the line **Issue a Refund**.
- At the next page, click on the line near the top, **Search your Payments transactions**.
- The next step forces you to log into your account (if you're not already at that point).
- Then, all you have to do is search through the sales you've made – Amazon provides a very helpful database tool – and when you find the right one, click on its **Transaction ID/Order ID** number.
- If the information that comes up confirms that it's the one you're after, then click **Refund** and you'll be walked through the last bits of information needed to credit the amount back

to the customer.

Simple, really.

If you have made recent sales, Amazon will take the refund amount from this accrual. Any excess will have to be debited to (taken from, that is) your bank account.

When transactions go bad

The "court of last resort" is Amazon's A-to-z Guarantee. Though Amazon will encourage the buyer and the seller in a failed transaction to work things out between them, this is the fallback position

If a buyer orders an item, and it never arrives, or it's substantially different from what they were expecting, they try to work things out with the seller for 30 days after the purchase. Then, the buyer has a 60-day window (a recent upgrade from 30 days) to make an A-to-z claim. Amazon looks over the claim, and decides what the buyer deserves in way of a refund. Essentially, the claim form is an agreement to accept whatever Amazon judges an appropriate settlement.

Amazon may absorb the cost of this refund, if they feel the customer was somehow wronged but cannot make a clear case that the merchant is at fault. If they feel it's clear that the seller has screwed up, the refund may be billed to that seller's account. In some cases, a seller has appealed this charge, and gotten some or all of it reversed.

So why would you as a merchant, want to mess around with the A-to-z Guarantee program? Simple: to bring in a third party to mediate a difficult situation. Let's say that someone buys a $100 book from you, then demands a refund when it doesn't arrive, even though you have a signed delivery receipt. Or you offer a refund when they return a book, and are sent something vastly different from the original item. If you make a good-faith effort to straighten things out with a buyer, and it quickly becomes apparent that things might be a bit odd, then you have the option to "boot the problem upstairs" and let Amazon get to the bottom of things. They'll probably ask you for your side of the story before making a final decision – though I've heard some quirky things about the process, like Amazon initiating a refund before investigating the claim, or giving a refund and telling the buyer to keep the item. All in all, it appears to be a step in the right direction, seeking a balance between keeping buyers happy and sellers honest, and an available option if you should need it.

If it comes down to the crunch, you can find the main page for filing an A-to-z Guarantee claim by a somewhat circuitous route. Go to the **Help** page, type **"a to z"** into the search box, choose **A-to-z Guarantee Protection**, and that'll bring you right to the page you want.

Remember, though, that Amazon frowns on merchants who have a regular parade of customers knocking on the door. On the other hand, a customer can only make a handful of A-to-z claims for the entire lifetime of their account, five in the Marketplace and three in Auctions and zShops. This might be a bargaining point when you are haggling with the buyer: "Do you really want to use one of your claims just to settle a $5 dispute?"

Post feedback

In almost every sale, you ought to give your buyer five stars out of five. This isn't as critical for buyers as for sellers, but there are bibliophiles like me who buy enough items on Amazon that the numbers add up – or, in this case, the average stays very close to 5. Thanks to Amazon Payments, it's almost impossible for a customer to place an order and then to cancel payment. If that customer has bought a few items from you, and they someday decide to look at their About me page, they will be pleasantly surprised to find that you consider them a valued customer and are willing to tell the world about it – and it's possible that, as the only merchant to do so, your little company shines like a spotlight. Feedback takes less than a minute, and is a really inexpensive way of setting your business up for potential repeat business and word-of-mouth reputation in the future. In other words, it may count for nothing, but a tiny effort could have eventual benefits.

In the event that the customer has been an absolute pain, you still ought to give them the benefit of the doubt. It costs you nothing except maybe a minor bruise to your ego.

But if you have a strong belief that this customer has, say, demanded a refund for an order they probably received, then say so. Don't get accusatory – just mention that the item was lost in the mail, that's all. If the buyer racks up a few of these "lost" orders, every merchant afterward will be a little more wary of a refund request for a mysteriously misplaced package. When you enter these subtle warnings, you encourage other Amazon sellers to follow suit. Plus, the vast bulk of buyers who don't pull these rare scams have a better selection and are less vulnerable to the cynicism of burned merchants. Everyone benefits who ought to.

Leaving feedback for a customer is (of course) simple. Click your **Account** button, choose **Your seller account**, then at Amazon.com Marketplace under View items click **sold**. Each entry has, in the lower-right corner, a little text reminder, **Please remember to leave feedback**. (After you actually do this, the message will be changed to Thank you for leaving feedback.) Choose a number – preferably **5 (Excellent)**, of course! – then fill in as laudatory a comment as you can manage and click **Submit feedback**. Your feedback will be flagged as being from a seller, so that it stands out from their own list of buyer feedback.

When your orders start to pick up, you can post your feedbacks one after the other. If you've got even a slow Internet connection, you can post at least two of these per minute, so it's not as though it's adding a major burden to your overhead.

To track, or not to track – don't stalk your customers!

There are some Amazon merchants that record the addresses of their customers, then send them advertising. Some of these people are quite sweet, and put out folksy e-mail newsletters about their real-world stores. On the other hand, some merchants sell the customer's information, apparently thinking that buying a book or CD constitutes what's called an "opt in" permission.

For the most part, don't do this. Resist the temptation. You might make a few cents per name from your customer list, but you won't make friends. Usually, you'd just come across as participating in yet another spam campaign. Anti-spam laws are unlikely to get any looser, and you could find that this use turns out to be grossly illegal at some point. Better that you don't develop the habit in the first place.

You can take advantage of this. A small note in fine print on your packing slip and e-mail could say something like "We do not believe in invading the privacy of our customers, and will not sell or share the information that you give us." By doing this, you are also helping to set a high standard for other merchants.

At most, you might want to keep a brief file. Many customers would enjoy a hand-written note on their packing slip, saying something like, "Hello again! Thank you for coming back, and we hope to find more merchandise that you will enjoy!" When they foray out shopping online, what could it hurt if they were a tiny bit more likely to check your selection first?

Getting the Edge, part II: pushing

You need to get the attention of the Amazon.com customer before you can sell them anything. Most of the time, they are browsing around with a pretty good idea of what they want, searching by title or digging through the listings for a favorite author. Many times, though, they are exploring a topic or category, maybe rooting around by keywords. Most of the items they look at are not what they want, and they are acting much like an customer in a real-world store, picking things off the shelf, flipping through the pages, and deciding whether this suits their immediate needs or, failing that, is something they would like to read anyway.

Part of the Amazon software behemoth looks at what you're looking at, compares the pages you chose to view with what other people looking at that entry also viewed, then pops up with little hints and suggestions like Customers that bought this item also bought... and You might also like... listings. Speaking as a regular Amazon customer myself, I use these suggestions infrequently, but they have directed me to an occasional forgotten gem or something I didn't even know had been published.

If you want to expend a little effort, you can bump the odds up a little for your items. While it's true that you may have to share the benefit with others listing the same title, you ought to be taking every boost to your margin if the method suits your skills. Once you get the hang of it, you will also have a better idea as to which targets simply aren't going to be worth the extra work, or when five minutes might all but guarantee a quick sale. As an added bonus, you might pick up some reputation as a trustworthy authority in your own right – it won't make you money, but it's good for the ego.

These entries require some information about you, and a decision or two such as the name you would like your feedback to be attributed to. The effort at that stage is minimal.

The Reviews attract buyers

Many items on Amazon.com, especially older ones, have no description whatever. The main entry is empty, and all available information barely fills a single browser window. Newer entries might have a few quotes from professional reviewers, a "review" comment made by the author or publisher (these are identifiable by their *zero-star ratings*, as they're not factored into the Average customer rating number, 1-5 stars, that each book gets), and quotes from the jacket blurbs. Older items were apparently entered in the early stages of Amazon before all these frills appeared, or it simply wasn't worth someone's time to obtain detail, and the entries have never been updated.

It wasn't worth Amazon's effort, but they have been gracious enough to leave a few doors open for you to do this.

This doesn't mean that you need to go all smarmy or namby-pamby or gushy about an item. Customers like it if *someone* says *something* about a book or CD. Once, we listed a book, which made me remember how much I absolutely despised it. I went in and utterly slagged the book, its first (and to date only) review. I think I got feedback of something like "7 out of 59 customers found this review helpful." But I also noticed that, when I went back with morbid curiosity to see how many people hated my review, more than half of the copies available on the Marketplace had vanished.

This baffled me for some time. I mean, I shred the thing and it *sells*? Eventually, I figured out that it was because there'd previously been no information about the book. I might be evil, but I'm also articulate and thorough.

Many of us have lousy memories. We remember that we treasured or detested a book, but we're a little foggy about things like the author, the title, the publisher, the year, and that sort of thing. Anyone who's worked in a bookstore knows the common plaint: "You know, the one with the blue cover! Anyway, I *think* it's blue. You tell me, you're the big-shot bookseller!"

I did some dirt on the book; true enough. However, I gave

enough detail about its contents that more than a dozen people said to themselves, "Oh, yeah – I remember that one!" and gave me a thumbs-down before going off to buy it. My ranting sparked their memory, and gave them an emotional attachment to the item.

Since then, I've also gone to the listings for certain CDs that I enjoy, and given brief reviews, excerpts from the liner notes (including more extensive parts from the LP if these were missing or indecipherable on the CD), and complete track listings if those weren't there. Again, I noted that sales of existing items increased. Many times, we remember only a snippet of a chorus, and if such information isn't on the Amazon.com entry, people dither, or move on to purchases about which they're more confident.

If you have any talent at all for writing or reviewing, then say something about the item you have, *especially* if

- there is no other description or review
- yours is the only listed item, or one of a handful
- you have more than one
- your item is especially collectible (unopened; limited edition; autographed)

If you don't have the talent, find someone who does. Surely you can at least lay hands on an articulate friend who can crank out the occasional informative hundred-word essay.

Customer Recommendations

On many Amazon.com entries, down below Product Details (and Look Inside This Book, if the item has that feature), you'll see a box which could be labeled one of two things. If it's something that hasn't been a hot item in recent memory, this section will be titled What's your Advice?, which usually means that nobody's made a recommendation yet. If the item has had some buzz, the title will be Our Customers' Advice followed by two recommendations: the book most often recommended *in addition to* that item by customers, and the book most often recommended *instead of* it.

The way you participate in this is really not mysterious or even difficult. If it's the second version of the Advice area, click on **Recommend an item!** and you'll get the same **I**

recommend panel as the first. There, you'll see a box for an item's ASIN (the Amazon Standard Identification Number that they use to catalogue every product listed on the site), and two choices:

- in addition to this product
- instead of this product

Getting the ASIN takes a little effort, but is easy enough once you get the hang of it. Having multiple browser windows open simplifies matters. Just use one window to find the entry that you are recommending, copy the ASIN that Amazon uses – either from the item's Product Details area or clipped directly from the page's address immediately after the "/ASIN/" part; it's ten characters long, made up of numeric digits and possibly a few letters – then paste it in the box provided at the entry where you want to flag customers down.

I've used this (as a fan) to send customers for CDs to titles by members of the band who've gone solo, and to point out books the author published under a pseudonym. As a customer, I've used this information to browse highly recommended items, and just to take a moment to glance at something that sounded interesting.

The Lists

Customers at Amazon.com are encouraged at every turn to put together their own lists of books they recommend for people interested in a particular subject. You can quickly turn this into your personal book-review page, packed with small thumbnail images of each book you mention. (And the same goes for CDs, videos, and a host of items. Ever wanted to take issue with Gene Siskel? Now's your chance!)

For the most part, this is an exercise in egotism, and I don't think that's a bad thing. You get a chance to speak your mind, justify your opinions, and occasionally admit to guilty pleasures in a semi-public forum. Unlike individual reviews under specific entries, you have the opportunity to present your authority in a unified chunk and demonstrate your range, looking a little less like a loser who owns only one DVD and watches it twice a day. And you also have the satisfaction of knowing that you are spreading your quirky tastes to others, eventually infecting the entire planet and bringing civilization as we know it to an end.

Aside from ego, these lists offer a nice bit of public-relations potential for sellers who have a real-world presence, without requiring you to post all this stuff on your own webpages or bury it somewhere in your on-line diary or weblog. (And unlike your personal site, you've already got a few thousand people an hour wandering past who might stop by for a browse.) I have found my Amazon reviews quoted on at least ten other sites – this is probably illegal, but with the free publicity for Amazon.com, for the item, and for me, nobody seems to be complaining.

If you want to turn your own reviews to your advantage, you could set up one page on your site that lists the titles and subjects of your assorted Amazon.com lists, then send potential customers directly to the list. If you put out a newsletter for your store, you can mention the new Amazon lists that you have added recently, or spool out the entire catalogue to date. If your writing is halfway decent, your customers can't help but pick up the impression that you really are expert in your trade. And those lists will remain accessible for a long, long time, perhaps for the lifespan of Amazon.com itself. Your legacy will outlast all your problems with servers and shaky Internet service providers and weblog hosts that sometimes disappear without warning along with all your writing.

And if your sales are mostly restricted to the Amazon route, creating a list is a great way of tying popular titles to rarer items that you have. To make up an example, let's say that you have a small cache of books that explain complicated physics to the lay reader. Though there are listings for them all in Amazon, who's going to even know the titles exist? Well, that's where your list would come in. When someone like Stephen Hawking comes out with a new book, you come up with a list to append to its Amazon page that mentions some of his previous works, plus a good short-list of anything from Einstein to Gleick to Feynman – and, by happy coincidence, the obscure items that you just happen to have available. A customer who is interested in Hawking's latest is also highly likely to be curious about similar subjects, as well as to speak to people with that sort of interest, so every such list that you put up is added potential for sales.

Submitting corrections

This is the area where you can help to make Amazon.com a better place for buyers and sellers alike. More than a few entries, especially for older items, are utterly mangled. The item is listed under the author's first or middle name, or by its subtitle. Sometimes the credit goes to the illustrator or whoever wrote the introduction. Or the spelling is simply so atrocious that anyone searching for the correct title will miss it entirely.

I was looking for a CD that I enjoy, hoping to send a copy to a friend. Searching out music CDs is usually faster than digging for books, so I was baffled when I couldn't find it by title or by performer. When I finally managed to dig it out by its barcode, I found that the entry didn't have the musician's name at all, and was listed under the French title. Obviously, I stormed in with corrections, and for good measure used the Recommendation feature to add explicit links to the musician's other CDs.

Whether you've got the item right in front of you or you just happen to have better information that whoever made the entry, then fix it. The methods are simple, and most only require a little clicking.

If you go to any entry on Amazon.com, and scroll down toward the bottom, you'll find a clearly defined area titled Suggestion Box. The only line that should concern you begins "Product information is incorrect" – the other stuff is helpful, but nowhere near as important. On the right end of this line, click **Online Catalog Update Form**.

The system will almost always give you a Sign In page that asks you to log in, or rather to clearly identify yourself and give your Amazon password. I've entered dozens of corrections in a single sitting, and I'm usually asked to log in each time; we're unsure if this is due to a glitch in the software that doesn't properly remember that you did this five minutes ago, or if Amazon is simply being extremely cautious – if it's the former, this will no doubt be changed in the future. In any case, if the box shows your correct e-mail address, simply type your Amazon account's password into the "Yes" box below, then click the long **Sign in using our secure server** button. (If this is the first time you've ever interacted with Amazon other than browsing, then tick the "No, I am a new customer" button and give the system your basic information.)

The next screen (assuming you've logged in correctly) is helpfully titled Amazon.com Online Catalog Update Form. Click **enter your corrections** on the next line.

The page that appears is somewhat redundantly headed Welcome to the Amazon.com Online Catalog Update Form. This offers you a list of the sorts of information for which you can offer corrections. Usually, all you'll want to mess with are the title or the name of author, but you can repair or add information to clean up obvious gaps and gaffes that you notice have gotten attached to that ISBN. Tick all of them that apply to your item's entry, then click **Continue**.

Here's the page where the action is. If the author's name is mangled beyond comprehension, tick the Delete name box at the end of the line – don't be too hasty, though, as there are misspellings that are commonly searched for, especially if the author has a highly unusual name. Enter the correct spelling in one of the Corrected author: spaces. If you have a long title that needs just minor repair, you can save yourself time by using your mouse to highlight the existing title, copy-and-paste it to the box below, then make the correction.

When you've completed the changes you want to see, click on the **Confirm** button. This brings up a screen that asks you to approve your editing. If there's something you've overlooked, click the **Edit corrections** button to go back and fix it. Otherwise, click the **Submit Update** button, and you're done.

Thanks!

These changes don't go through automatically, otherwise the entries would be vulnerable to more mistakes being added by well-meaning but inept customers. The folks at Amazon.com will review your work, and in most cases post the changed information within two or three days. Once in a while, our corrections seem to get lost in the shuffle, so we enter them again and they go through.

Find fun fixing facts

Sometimes, things are confusing. We had an item where the author's first name on the jacket is "Alexei" (as it's spelled on entries for all of his other books), but the Amazon entry was only for "Alexeyeev" (which is what the Library of Congress entry has, too). Neither one is really *wrong*, just confusing. We entered the Anglicized spelling and left the other one alone. Occasionally, Portuguese and Spanish names can confuse the system because of the magnificent lists of surnames, and Arabic and Chinese names can be worse. Your job is not to get all the snarls out, just to go for the overlooked obvious: what it says on the jacket.

Another fault of the software is titles and authors that have been entered in some language other than English. A reasonably smart word-processor program accepts complicated characters like tildes, umlauts, and accent marks. Amazon's software doesn't qualify as "smart" in this respect. The result is that a single character from everyday French has exploded into a mishmash of three characters – a simple word with a cedilla and an accent or two becomes a long, meaningless string of letters with a few numbers and punctuation marks – which makes that word totally unsearchable for us boring Americans who stubbornly type in the basic 26 letters and ignore the funny marks.

When you are browsing through entries, and you see something that's obviously wrong, please take two minutes to straighten it out. As I say, everyone benefits.

I'll admit that I get a cheap thrill from this task. I spent a quiet evening fixing every *Jhonson* and *Smiht* entry I could find, and straightening out titles that had hilarious confusions between *desert* and *dessert* (I doubted that *Easy French Deserts* was correct, though I was ready to find out what *Dessert of the Damned* was all about).

Handy little details

There are a few things that will make your Marketplace more pleasant. You probably won't use them often, but they can be terribly convenient.

Changing your Account Options

This can get a little confusing sometimes, because options are divided up between your Amazon account and your Seller Account. In general, you might want to ensure that you have a personal account that is entirely separate from business.

The fastest way to get there is that persistent **Account** button lurking at the top-right of the page, which takes you to (thankfully) a paged titled Your Account. This is primarily your "personal" information – a little confusing since a company would have the same sort of page. The top part of the page gives you as a customer much control over tracking your purchases, including returning items for a refund. If you scroll down, you'll find links ready to help you change things like the e-mail address to which Amazon sends notifications, which of those notifications you want to receive in the first place, the credit card (or cards) you use to place orders, or the criteria that Amazon uses when recommending items for you based on your browsing and buying habits.

Off on the right is a smaller column, the top box of which is for Auctions, zShops, and Marketplace. Click on the second choice, **Your seller account**. This brings up a page with some of your most necessary actions. The fifth heading down, **Your Seller Account**, offers all sorts of options to change the settings to your Marketplace merchant account. The big exception would be your banking information, which is just above that: under Get Paid, click **View your Amazon Payments account and billing history**, then choose **Edit your Amazon Payments account settings**.

Basically, if you want to change something but can't find on this page, chances are that you can't change it.

Using Amazon to track your account

While we're on the Your Amazon Payments Account page, notice that you have two other choices, to **Search your Payments transactions** or to **View your Amazon Payments account summary**. They are slightly different ways of combing through your transactions, and whichever you use will depend on what information you need, your working style, and your mood.

The second ("View") choice gives you the option to download your two-week statement so that you can paste it into your bookkeeping system. Choose **Export This Statement** at the top of the page, and the data will be sent to you in a tab-delimited format for easy inclusion in a spreadsheet.

The first ("Search") option lets you specify which of your orders you would like to see, and then to download this as a file – this is incredibly handy for tax purposes, and lets you move your business up to a formal bookkeeping system at some future time without having to enter all this data manually. Just choose **Export Transactions** and the file will begin transmitting to your computer.

If you're handy enough with technology that this sort of thing is a snap, you might want to look further into the possibilities for automating some of your recordkeeping.

Going on Vacation

My little company frequently likes to take time off. This is usually for a vacation, when we don't want the people left behind to be swamped by Amazon orders on top of their other duties. Sometimes, things are so hectic around the office that none of us wants one more distraction until the dust starts to settle.

This is easy to do: **YOUR ACCOUNT**, **Your seller account**, then under Your Seller Account click **Update your Vacation Settings**. Click on the obtrusive orange **Begin your vacation** button and your account will be safely locked within 36 hours (generally much less). When you're done slacking off, return and click the orange button again, and your listings will spring back to life after a similar wait.

Be a little cautious with the Vacation feature. Early in our venture, I told the system that we were shutting down for the holidays, and didn't think any more about it for almost a month. I later found that, between the time that I had made the request and the time it was actually processed by Amazon, a few dozen of our items had come up for relisting. Because we missed the window, we had to re-enter every item.

If I had noticed this at the time, fixing it would have been almost as inconvenient. We would have had to:

- request that our Vacation Setting status be returned to normal operation
- wait for that request to be processed – usually very prompt but Amazon says it can take up to 36 hours
- relist the items
- re-request our Vacation Settings
- hope that there were no more relistings that would come due while request was being processed

This also demonstrates a good reason to post your listings in big chunks with gaps of at least a few days between each chunk.

Closing your Marketplace presence

Once in a while, a Merchant might simply need to move along. The real-world store is closing, the Amazon experience takes up too much time or isn't profitable enough, or maybe the owners want to sell their Marketplace shop or change its image. How do you go about shutting the virtual doors?

Really, the long and the short of it is that you can't. Amazon has a policy of keeping many "placeholders" around, even if they're books that never went to press after a description page was created in the Marketplace, and they do much the same with Merchant accounts. Should you decide to pull up stakes and withdraw, your account may well end up being around for the life of the site. All you can really do is to delete your listings, strip information from your Storefront if you have one, and (hopefully) move on to bigger and better things.

The next step up

My company is very satisfied with our Amazon.com experience to date. We have established a nice little trade, picked up some valuable experience in Internet-based marketing, enjoyed a clear profit from our trickle of sales, and found a commercial excuse to indulge our passions for books and bargains.

Without too much effort, you can probably reach the same point in a few months. If your trade is booming, you might want to consider some ways offered by Amazon to expand your range. We haven't yet had the motivation, but let's take a look at the options.

Auctions

The simplest way to extend your reach on Amazon.com is to take advantage of the auction possibilities. This is very handy when you have an item that has no relevant listing on Amazon, or is highly collectible. This also gives you the option of selling older LPs and tapes that don't have their own listings but could be of interest to fans. I've seen classic posters, ticket stubs, teeshirts, and other promotional items sold this way.

If I were to do this on a regular basis, I would probably use a service such as eBay, but having it on Amazon gives you opportunity to draw greater attention for your auction item by tying its listing to those of other items.

Listing an item for auction costs 10¢. When it sells, Amazon collects a closing fee of 5% for items up to $25; this rate reduces slightly for more expensive items, so something up to $1,000 will have a fee of $1.25 (5% of the first $25) plus 2.5% of the remainder, and for items priced yet higher you would pay $25.63 plus 1.25% of the remainder.

There are also a few merchandising options available for your auction item. For $2/item, you can give your listing greater visibility (literally!) by having it presented in boldface. You can "bid for placement" (a minimum of 5¢/day per item), which raises placement of your listing closer to the top when potential customers are searching by category or subject – but be warned that, when there are a lot of similar items or other merchants who are bidding for the right, getting toward the top will cost you more. In any case, you can also "CrossLink" your listing to related items, so that customers browsing a description will see your Auction item as an option – the best part is, this option costs you nothing.

To learn more about auctions on Amazon, go to the Help area, click on the **Selling at Amazon.com** heading, and select (near the end of the list on the left) **Auctions**. This FAQ area will tell you everything you need to know (and then some!), including such handy minutiae as basics of editing HTML to maximize the visual impact of your item and its listing.

The zShops: easing the Amazon bite

Signing your business up for zShop status will cost you $39.99 per month for up to 40,000 item listings, which they call the **Pro Merchant Subscription**. (The Help listings hint that the zShops may at some point become an intermediate option between basic Merchant and Pro Merchant accounts, but for the moment they're pretty much the same thing. Technically, every merchant has something resembling a zShop, but it's the Pro Merchant status that makes this more than a generic page.) In exchange for the fee, you get a nice handful of benefits.

First of all, that monthly fee frees you from the extra 99 cents that Amazon takes from every basic Marketplace sale. If you have gotten to the point of consistently selling more than 40 books per month, then it makes perfect economic sense to make the leap for just this benefit.

The benefits don't stop there, though.

As with the Auctions, you have much more flexibility to list items that aren't available in the standard Amazon listings. I am a fan of the science fiction of R. Lionel Fanthorpe, who wrote more than fifty novels, none of which is recent enough to be listed, but I'd bet that there are at least a couple dozen available at any moment in the zShops.

If you have a zShop, you can put an item up for auction

without the 10¢/item listing fee that mere Merchants pay. Again, a small savings that can add up if you intend to have many auctions.

Having a zShop gives you access to further merchandising options, as with the Auctions. You greatly increase your opportunities for customer contact on Amazon by having a zShop account, which they call the **Storefront**. You can mess around with the colors of your Storefront page, and add your own logo and other graphics, sort of a super "About Me" page. Then you can use this page's URL in your own advertising, possibly from your own site or home page, which is especially handy if you are developing some sort of a niche or specialty; for instance, I know at least one little company that deals almost exclusively in collectible Ford manuals. If you'd like to see the classic entry-point for all Amazon zShops, try ***www.zShops.com*** to get a feel for the sort of company you'd keep.

The Pro Merchant closing fees are the same as for auctions (see above). Since my company's Amazon sales can be somewhat sporadic, we haven't made the Pro Merchant leap yet, but it grows more tempting with every sale. A book that is sold by an ordinary Merchant for $20 pays a $3.99 commission to Amazon. The same book sold by a Pro Merchant gives Amazon exactly $1.00. That's an extra $2.99 in your virtual pocket from a single sale. It wouldn't take many of those to earn back that $39.99/month, and everything after that is profit.

I do need to warn you that Amazon has standards to keep their site from being used for questionable business practices that would reflect badly on everyone. If your zShop begins to develop a history of issuing refunds for listing things you turn out not to have, or shipping items that are clearly not what your listing promised, they might opt to bill your account for the time they put into paperwork. Though they aren't explicit, a few comments on their site hint that they reserve the right to cancel your account if you look too shady. As always, be careful, and be businesslike.

Though they need your credit-card information to get started, your Amazon account will (hopefully) soon be carrying a balance, and their fees are deducted from this amount until it hits zero, and only then will fee amounts be put on your card.

Even with all these benefits to the Pro Merchant account,

there's more. Amazon makes available their **Inventory Loader** protocol. Many real-world merchants enter their used-book inventory into their store's computer by scanning the ISBN, which can lead to fantastic savings of effort and time (and thus money) when we're talking hundreds of books. Rather than having to go back and manually enter those items to Amazon, the Inventory Loader takes this database information and allows you to quickly upload and manage these as Amazon listings.

The zShop concept is a bit long in the tooth. It predates the Marketplace, and merchants generally feel that Amazon isn't supporting the zShop concept with an intention of phasing it out. But, for the moment at least, a zShop might be exactly what you want for displaying your wares in the best light, especially if a large portion of your inventory does not have listings in the standard Amazon pages. And the Pro Merchant account may prove to be the long-term legacy of the zShops concept.

To learn more about the Pro Merchant possibilities, go to the Help area, choose the **Selling at Amazon.com** heading, then **Experienced and Volume Selling**, and start with the very first entry, the **Pro Merchant Quick Start Guide**. Also, the Volume Listing Tools FAQs will give you much information on how you can both upload your items as one big chunk of data and accurately track your inventory and sales. (If this sort of high-tech approach suits you, then you might also want to check out AWS, **Amazon Web Services**. This is an ongoing Amazon project to see how much they can automate of their independent sellers' bookkeeping and inventory management. To learn more, go to the bottom of a page and click **Sell Items**, then scroll down to the bottom again for **Web Services**. There is also a discussion forum specific to AWS – look below at "Real live advice" for more about the boards.)

The Amazon Advantage program

As you go flipping through all the pages, you will regularly see many terms that have no meaning for you. That's fine, really; Amazon.com is a very big playground, getting bigger all the time, and it's unlikely that you will ever have need in this lifetime to use most of the options that are available.

Lately, though, I've encountered a few entrepreneurs who are atypical, but obviously not as rare as I had thought. One bunch owns a bookstore aimed at young adults, and has started publishing music CDs, with plans to found a magazine and possibly publish a few books. Another example is a small music publisher that wants to produce books as well.

So, let's take a brief look at the Amazon Advantage program.

If you are small publisher, it's surprisingly easy to put your products out on Amazon. I asked an editor at the publisher of this very book to walk me through the process, and I have to say that listing a book takes a few minutes, and even less if you cut-and-paste from information that you've already got in word-processor files.

Literally, the hardest part of the process is in getting started – and that's relatively simple, compared to setting up your Merchant account.

Understand, though, that your going live in the Advantage program puts Amazon at a little more of a risk than signing up yet another Marketplace merchant. A seller who screws up a handful of orders is easily discovered, and quickly banished. However, a publisher who turns out to be offering bogus or nonexistent merchandise, or whose product description page ends up being very misleading, could rapidly defraud Amazon customers of thousands of dollars, leaving the company looking extremely darned silly. Reasonably, Amazon.com doesn't want these sorts of smudges on their business reputation. Therefore, if you tell them that you want to sell your company's products on their website, Amazon is going to look you over a bit critically. So, you have to apply to Amazon, maybe supply further information, then wait for them to get around to approving your Advantage account.

Then, every time you list a new product, real human beings are going to actually sit down and examine your product description, possibly querying the Library of Congress, researching the ISBN or UPC you give them, running any questions that occur about patents and trademarks and copyrights past their legal department, and maybe looking at your company's Web presence – this process, my publisher assures me, can take up to three weeks. Someone from Amazon might contact you to "suggest" revisions. And once you have it up there, you can make corrections, and even some changes or updates, but if the product actually gets to market, then the product description page will stay forever on Amazon, so that the aftermarket sales have a correct page from which to sell.

Though you may never even have heard of the Advantage program, you've encountered it many times if you've used Amazon at all. Go to the home page (www.amazon.com, in case you forgot), scroll all the way down to the bottom, and one of the last choices will be **Join Advantage**. This takes you to a very nice FAQ page that is also a log-in point for Advantage members. You can read all about it, and even fill out an application from this point.

I don't want you to get the idea that Advantage is a panacea: assuming that Amazon even accepts your company and products, it'll cost you $29.95 a year, *plus* Amazon takes a hefty 55% of your selling price. (And you're limited to selling only "Books, Music & Video" products.) However, you probably don't know that this is a typical (and comparatively lenient, even) discount for any wholesaler or distributor. Amazon orders from you, then sends items out to individual buyers. The initial Amazon purchases will probably be three units at a time, but the size begins to increase as demand for your item picks up. What you're getting out of it is simplified order fulfillment, placement of your products in a world-wide, 24/7 catalogue that can be browsed, Googled, linked to related and similar products, and is generally more powerful and better looking than anything you could afford. You don't take the financial hit if a customer turns out to be running a forged identity or stolen credit card – Amazon takes their cut to absorb that risk.

Not for everybody, then, but possibly exactly what your business needs.

Associate selling

Down at the bottom of that same homepage, probably immediately before the "Join Advantage" tag, is **Join Associates**. Basically, if you already have a webpage or control of your own site, you can use this to drive customers to Amazon to make purchases.

For the most part, this is a way of building the Amazon customer base. True, the link you use to send people their way has a little notation on it, which tracks your Associate account, and credits you with a 9% cut of whatever that referred person happens to buy. (Last week, someone told me the commission used to be 15% – ah, progress!) Your payment gets sent out to you every three months.

I've met a few folks who are particularly able to benefit from Associate selling, and you might be in a similar position. For instance, there's an author whose book is long out of print. When the publishing company decided to stop supporting it, he bought the last 1,500 copies for a fraction of their SRP. This isn't really enough of an inventory to justify even attempting to join the Advantage program, but he can send potential customers over to his Marketplace listings, where he places a few of the perfect copies as New, some scuffed or dinged copies under Used, and one signed copy in Collectible. He gets his price (usually SRP for New copies) plus the 9%, and can also send his fans to a few related books and get those commissions as well.

As before, the Join Associates page is the point to sign up as well as the login point for participants to check their accounts.

Making a custom page for your items

Most merchants will not find it worth their time to go about creating special Amazon listings for their items. However, if you are selling your own publications but don't want to join the Advantage program, or you have an occasional high-end item, this might be worth your while, especially if you are already invested in the Pro Merchant program. As I write, this option is still in its evaluation stage, and may go through some drastic changes (or even elimination) in the future, but I want to take a moment to glance at it.

Creating a custom page gives Merchants an opportunity to go into detail about what they have to offer. Not only are potential customers given more information, but the page increases the chances that a customer will encounter this listing when they are searching or browsing for similar or related items. You have up to 2,000 characters to wax effusive about this product and entice the customer. If you are producing your own books, pamphlets, or CDs, this feature makes Amazon.com a fantastic addition to your self-promotion efforts, as well as providing a way to take orders and accept credit cards. (Within limits, of course – Amazon doesn't want to be accused of providing safe haven for people selling pirated software, bootlegged music, photocopied books, or outrageously offensive original materials. If you should cross these boundaries, expect to be having an official chat about your status as a merchant.) Further increasing the chances of getting a sale is the option to provide a graphical image, a photograph or piece of art, presumably of the product you are selling but possibly your company logo or something similar.

On the down side, the custom-page option is only available to Pro Merchants, it is restricted to less than half the standard Amazon categories – you can sell books or music, for instance, but not software or video games – the amount of effort is a little daunting for many people, and presently the construction features only run on Internet Explorer (version 5.0 or newer). Plus, once you finish a detail page, not only can you *not* change its product type or category – choose wisely! – but you cannot delete the page; it becomes part of the vast Amazon catalogue. You can always appeal this, but Amazon prefers to keep out-of-date product entries so that other merchants who are selling used items will have increased accuracy in the future.

If you want to find out more about this option, go to the Help area, click the heading **Selling at Amazon.com**, then look for the heading **Create a Product Page**. This would be a booklet in itself, and I don't want to go talking too far beyond my experience, possibly confusing the few people who would get around to using it.

Real live advice

Okay, I know that I'm not the brightest candle in the menorah, so I can admit the following. Maybe it'll give you a lot of help right when you need it, especially when you're starting out, and I wish I'd known about it before I had this book almost completed!

Amazon maintains a group of virtual forums. If you've never used something like this on the Internet, this is a perfect time to learn.

- Go to the top-right of a screen and choose **Help**.
- Down the left side, after the "Ordering" and "Gifts & Gift Certificates" sections will be

Selling at Amazon.com. Click on this heading.

- In the right-hand column of the box, about halfway down is a bullet-point for **Announcement and Discussion Boards**. (Though you really ought to read every article in this list at least once, believe me.)
- This will take you to four more bullet-points, of which you want the top-left choice, **Seller Discussion Boards** – though, again, find time to read the other choices, too.

And this leaves you at a list of descriptions for the five Seller boards.

- Help for New Sellers
- Listing Management & Reports
- Shipping, Feedback & Returns
- Third-Party Software & Services
- Seller Soapbox

Start out with the first, of course. In reality , if you say something like, "Hi, we just started our Marketplace account last week," you'll at least get directions to relevant discussion threads – though I hope you'll forgive the occasional "oh, not *that* one again!" response, since some questions really do resurface every few days.

For the most part, the last of the list, the Seller Soapbox, is where all the action is. There is a lot of discussion unrelated to Amazon.com business, generally marked "OT" (for "off-topic") in the thread's title. The various sellers complain to each other, ask for advice about problems, or trade tips and suggestions for improving their Marketplace sales and business in general.

The forums are monitored by Amazon employees, and occasionally lead to official responses, changes in procedures and site design, and even crackdowns against sellers who appear to be fraudulent or irresponsible.

Software to improve business

Okay, since someone asked. If you want to learn more about various programs and packages that will allow you to track or even automate some (or more) of your Marketplace selling experience, then I know pretty much nothing and I would never speak out for (and rarely against) something with which I don't have first-hand experience.

If you would like to look into this, even if merely to satisfy your curiosity, stop in at the aforementioned **Third-Party Software and Services** discussion forum. They are for the most part lovely and helpful people, and will gladly throw their opinion and experience out for discussion.

Personally, I use Excel and Word, and I don't upload or download our Amazon data. If you want to try getting all fancy, get good advice, then go ahead – but first, read the next chapter.

New toys to consider

In 2003, I speculated that there might be room to bring technological advances to bear, to aid our business. For instance, downloading to my Palm all the Amazon listings of items that customers have expressed interest in, along with what condition of item they're looking for and how much they're willing to pay. (You'll notice on the main page for some items a note to the effect 7 buyers waiting! in the MORE BUYING CHOICES box.) People thought I was putting far too much effort into this whole Amazon thing.

The world, as usual, has gone shooting past me. I won't name any names, because I'm still not sure I want to plug this, but I can tell you about the system.

Basically, you use an Internet-enabled cellphone to access your account with a company. You enter a book (usually by its ISBN), and the software digs through various on-line sales sites and gives you an idea of what that book is worth. Depending on the company you go with, a subscription to this service

Some people go the low-tech route, using the cellphone to read the information off to someone at home who pores over the listings

The first problem with this is that it encourages the user to not use intelligence. There are already stories of entrepreneurs spending hours scanning every Danielle Steele and Steven King paperback they come across, rather than focusing on volumes that actually have some sales potential. I've heard of one searcher who lost interest in any book without an ISBN because their software couldn't handle it, and passing up one eminently resellable book after another.

Secondly, such cherry-picking doesn't reflect the ebb-and-flow of the used-book market. For instance, say that you reject a book because its listings tell you that there are five available on

Amazon in the $10 range, and the one you're holding would cost you $8. Hardly worth it if you're going for a "quick kill" sale, yet someone else might list it at $25, and sell it in a month. And as anyone who's been doing Amazon-type sales for a while can tell you, today's glutted title can be next-week's pricey rarity.

A good trader has at least a bit of a gambler's talent. I regularly bring home 40 books, then find that a quarter of them are hardly worth listing, and up to half will have to wait weeks or months to fetch a good price – but I only rarely harvest a book that's worth less on Amazon than I paid for it, and I do that with what amounts to educated guessing. A handy device cannot replace a finely trained intuitive ability.

Increasingly, bookstores and some auction sites are asking that their customers not spend the entire afternoon chatting on the telephone when most of shoppers enjoy a more properly morgue-like (okay, *library*-like) atmosphere for their shopping experience.

All in all, if you actually know books, and you are willing to keep up with the market beyond the demand of the moment, this sort of enabled cellphone could be a valuable tool. I suspect that most users are intending to get rich quick without much effort (see the next chapter for more on this attitude), and the majority will simply fritter their money away faster thanks to the technology. If you are just starting out in Internet sales, or know little or nothing about the book market, my stern advice is to get as sharp as you can before relying on such crutches, or (to continue the metaphor) you'll never learn how to walk. If this sort of service catches on, you'll be competing only for the quick-kill sales, and not for long-term profitability – having your own kernel of intelligence gives you a clear advantage over someone who simply has money to burn.

Free money?

There is a phenomenon taking place on Amazon that does not strike me as particularly honest, and its abuse has gone a long way toward dragging down customer confidence in all Amazon.com transactions, whether purchasing from the company itself or from any of its thousands of sellers.

It looks like an easy way to make money, for only a little work. You don't have to lay out cash for inventory or pack a single item. All you do is list stuff, set the prices, and cash the checks.

Drop shipping

This is primarily for new items. You find yourself a distributor (some publishers may be willing to sell as well) and convince them that you are a retail outlet. Then you go through their listings and choose which items you want to enter on Amazon.com, setting the price at whatever you think the market will bear. When an Amazon customer orders from you, simply take their information and use it to place an order with the distributor, giving out the customer data as the shipping address. Since distributors typically sell new items for 40% off the list price, you can offer as much of a discount as you think you can spare from that margin. In fact, if you have a strong belief in your marketing skills, you are free to ask for more than SRP.

It's just that simple. The money flows into your Amazon account, you place an order for the requested item at (hopefully) less than you were paid, someone else does the rest of the work, and you pocket the difference. Should you have access to programming skills, I imagine that there are ways for the Amazon order to be automatically rewritten and sent to your distributor

If you work with a company that is in your business's state, then you likely will have to provide your state-issued tax identification number, in order to demonstrate that you are purchasing items for resale, and therefore shouldn't be required to pay your state's sales tax on these items. Choose a company from another state, and you may not have to even work that hard.

Of itself, drop shipping is an honest method of extending the availability of items. Drop shippers who works with reputable wholesalers and distributors – who are diligent about putting out orders swiftly, who do not list what they do not actually have on hand, and who maintain a stringent level of quality control – are worthy competitors in the Marketplace.

List loading

This is a little newer than drop shipping, and can cover items that are currently in press or for which the distributor has acquired an inventory of overstocks and cutouts (thus including out-of-production titles), or even just everyday used items.

The wholesaler makes up a list of current inventory, usually as a spreadsheet, then makes this available (in an e-mail attachment or on a webpage). Amazon sellers can take this list, choose the entries they want to post, specify the prices they want to get, then upload their whole imaginary catalogue using the Amazon Web Services (AWS) tool or the Book Loader. (To learn more about this, go to the Selling at Amazon.com area of Help, Choose **Experienced and Volume Selling**, then **Volume Listing Tools**.)

However, many distributors make these lists available merely as a convenient point of reference to retailers. When they put these lists out, they make the tacit assumption that a buyer for a real-world store understands that a particular title may be out of stock, perhaps permanently, when they place an order, and that recent high-tech inventions like the telephone are necessary tools to ensure that it can still be had.

Often without permission, shady Amazon dealers (Marketplace and zShops alike) take these lists, add a substantial profit margin onto the prices, then automatically upload the information to Amazon as though this were their own available inventory.

How this goes wrong

Of itself, drop shipping isn't in the least crooked. However, it's sometimes readily seen as a "magic money machine" by individuals with questionable scruples, or a propensity for ineptitude, or both. Let me illustrate.

I had the (mis)fortune to experience this on one of my first Amazon.com purchases, which also shows that the problems are hardly limited to freelance boobs. I ordered a used copy of a reasonably popular CD. Skipping the absolute bargains at the low end of the scale, I decided to pay the extra dollar to buy from A Major Retail Chain that has a large selection of used and overstock items – with their Feedback list over 13,000 at the time, it seemed like a good idea.

A few minutes later, I received an e-mail thanking me effusively for my order, and assuring me that the CD would be shipped the moment they found a copy in one of their stores.

That should have been warning enough.

A week later, an e-mail assured me that they were still diligently searching for that CD, which simply had to be around somewhere.

Days later, another such e-mail.

When one more note arrived, assuring me that the clever disc would not elude them much longer, what with their massive database network and all, I canceled my order at Amazon.com and requested a refund.

I'm willing to be charitable and agree that A Major Retail Chain is not dishonest, just entirely too stupid to participate in Internet marketing. But if *they* can't get it right – in fact, they clearly had a whole set of procedures in place to deal with this problem, hinting that I was hardly the first – then I have to believe that many of the people who set up similar (though smaller scale) schemes because they pick up the smell of easy money aren't going to be diligent enough to do a whole lot better.

Merely because a distributor has a title on their price list doesn't mean that it is actually available. Even with current titles, the publisher could be entirely out of stock, and accruing back orders before committing to another print run, thus reducing their own risk of overreaching the actual demand, while keeping their profit margin up by assuring as big a run as necessary. (This happens all the time in publishing.) The distributor could have a bias toward dealing with its full-case orders first, working down toward single-item shipments, and possibly selling all its copies of a title before getting anywhere near the order for the hapless Amazon customer.

I'm not making this up. I know of a few titles that, for whatever reasons, were never actually published, yet somehow ended up with an Amazon listing. There are two or three drop-shippers that claim to have these for sale, which is physically impossible.

Abusing the customer

It is sometimes possible to spot a drop-shipper because they describe a book they clearly don't have sitting in front of them. Descriptions like "May be ex-library or have small remainder mark" or "All books are listed as good. Most books very good or better" are giveaways. Some of the least scrupulous make notations like "OUR EDITION MAY VARY," meaning that the item they're listing is probably in the wrong place – an excellent opportunity to abuse the trust of an unwary student believing that, having found the correct Amazon entry for a textbook, all Marketplace books are correctly identified.

Of course, Marketplace sellers are not the only culprits. I frequent another site where the detailed description of a certain hard-to-find book makes it very clear that up to six sellers have listed the same unique item, though I suppose it's *possible* that the only six available in the world have identical faults (and identical descriptions of them).

Customers check the Marketplace because they are led to believe that an item listed there is available and ready to ship immediately. Since drop shippers (honest and elsewise) are not flagged as such and their item listings look like everyone else's, the customer is clueless to understand which seller actually possesses an item and will have it on the way in days or even hours, and which are selling potentially empty promises. This especially irritates a customer who is purchasing for a class or for a gift; if you sift through the feedback listings of certain sellers, you might note an irate student who had to drop out of a course, or even failed it outright, because a promised textbook never arrived, or was an outdated edition that had been sold as the current version – at, of course, new-book prices.

When a customer gets burned in such a transaction, they can and will take it out on all Marketplace sellers. Surprisingly, some buyers do not understand that all those items are actually offered by thousands of sellers who may never cross each other's paths in this lifetime. You'll find your Feedback rating sacked because their book (shipped by standard mail) took more than five days to arrive. Some sellers report that they have received awful feedback ratings within *minutes* of a purchase. Often, such anger and frustration has been caused by a failed interaction with a drop shipper.

A retailer who orders an item from a distributor runs the risk that an occasional item will be out of stock at the warehouse, and that a new shipment is on the way and will be mailed to the seller as soon as it arrives. Having run a real-world store that specialized in small-press books, I would say that this happened at least once a month. Unless this was a special request by a customer, the delay was no big thing: when you have books, you sell them, and when you don't, there are plenty of other items to fill the shelves.

However, Amazon is different – supposedly. When a customer makes a Marketplace purchase, they are assured on every single entry that the item offered "Usually ships in 1-2 business days." In their explanation of a Marketplace seller's responsibilities, Amazon clearly says:

> **Please note that sellers must ship within two days of the purchase.**

(The specific page is under Help >> Selling at Amazon.com >> Fulfillment, Getting Paid and Feedback >> Fulfillment and Shipping Credits.) Nowhere is there an amendment that says, "…unless you are reordering through someone else," or "…but it's okay if you add a note that says you will take longer." If it's sold through the Amazon Marketplace, the item has to be on its way in two business days from the initial order – period.

All in all, I cannot accept (to borrow from Orwell) that, where the same set of rules is clearly stated as applying equally to *all* Marketplace sellers, some sellers are apparently more equal than others.

Technology versus intelligence

I want to briefly mention a complicated way for sellers to tweak Marketplace prices. This is a sort of brokering or forcing (these are addressed in the next chapter), but it fits more properly into a discussion of slightly shady practices that can readily go awry.

There are "spider" programs available on the Internet that comb through the books listed by various on-line sites like Amazon. Depending on the complexity of the spider, it can return a surprising amount of useful data, which is then matched up with an Amazon bulk listing facility such as Inventory Loader. If the spider is used on Amazon, the data can note the lowest price of a given title, the average price, and the highest price. A seller who uses this software can then hand it off to other software that goes in and relists their items competitively. Unfortunately, "competitive" might mean "set my item's price three cents lower than the current cheapest." At first glance, this seems to be a really slick way of automatically holding the bottom price. But when more than one seller is using this method on a particular title, their spiders lock into a downward cycle, and pretty soon they are slugging it out at the absolute bottom as one-cent books, meaning that the seller will lose money if it actually sells before they tell their software to knock off. When you realize that some of these sellers are running their spiders over the Amazon listings a few times a day, the chaos level can be stunning. Less often, the spiders will lock into a fight for the highest price, usually if the item is very scarce. This can have a purpose: if the seller actually has a copy of the title, a glut of insanely high-priced listings makes their real book (priced fairly) appear to be a bargain.

The power of the spiders isn't limited to Amazon, though. There are dozens of other websites that can be searched. Once in a while, one of these inept brokers will notice that an item unavailable on Amazon.com (or unusual enough to be high priced) will appear on one of these other sites for a few dollars. The seller decides to drop ship this item, listing it on Amazon without actually buying it. Again, this works okay as long as only one seller does it – unless it sells on the other site first, of course, which often results in an Amazon buyer getting a dodgy "sorry, that item is temporarily out of stock" e-mail days or weeks after purchase. But if another spider-using seller comes up with the same scheme, their software can lock horns in a rapidly spiraling (upward or downward) battle for the listing that actually sells. When a few more sellers join the fight, the whole thing gets ridiculous to anyone who knows what's going on.

In the Amazon forums, I've read posts by two sellers who delight in sometimes killing these bidding wars. They scan other sites until they find the item that they're certain is the bone of contention, then buy it. While those ridiculously inflated prices are still listed, they put the item up on Amazon at a reasonable profit, and sell it quickly. Once in a while, they even purchase the item from one of those bogus Amazon listings, then leave scathing feedback when they're told it doesn't exist. A little extreme, yeah, but sometimes more entertaining than any "reality" television.

Some sellers are clearly using software that's smarter than they are. One Marketplace seller (who I really ought to name, but I'll restrain myself) listed a fresh load of used books. Then, having some bizarre change of heart, they changed their prices. Then changed them again. And again.

I noticed this because every price change was still actively listed. This seller clearly hadn't had the sense to purge the old listings before entering the new ones.

In the end, each of these books was listed at least five times, priced at $2.95, $3.95, $4.75, $4.95, and $8.85. This only came to my attention because I was about to enter one of our own items, which I knew to be somewhat obscure, and Amazon had only had one other copy available the previous day – but suddenly there were six more, all from the same Marketplace seller. This is, to say the least, unusual. Later in the day, listing another item, I found that the same seller claimed to have five, with the same strange pricing. I was so intrigued by this that I found more than 40 instances before I gave up.

The only thing that gave this away, really, was the strange spread in prices. Others are likely doing the same thing, and making the same mistake, just more subtly.

Inherent problems

The overriding danger of Internet-based drop shipping is that, to make it work, sellers need to be extremely cautious about creating imaginary books. Consider a "multiple listing service" called something like **Evil Empire Books**. Now, EEB doesn't have any books of its own, merely taking a fee from real-world bookstores and Internet sellers to list their items at a central site. All well and good, thus far: as a book nut, I frequent four of these sites myself, and it's very convenient to be able to search all around the world from a single site, with all the prices and descriptions laid out in front of me for comparison.

Sometimes, one small seller might have an actual item, followed by listings culled from two other services to whom that seller has agreed to pay a fee. These are each in turn listed by (say) two other sellers that are freelance drop shippers. All of these have accounts with EEB. The result is that there are now up to 18 listings on EEB alone – and only one book that actually exists. If another site gets into the game, the number jumps again. When that single beleaguered book sells, anyone who buys one of the other listings is almost guaranteed to get a "temporarily out of stock" notice weeks or even months later (unless one seller along the way is shrewd enough to locate another copy).

Let's say that you go to Amazon, and buy a book from Bob, who happens to be a drop shipper. Bob takes your order, then buys the book from Fred, specifying that it should be sent to you. Fred, however, is a drop shipper as well, and orders it from Julius. This chain could go on for quite some length, with each reseller making only a few cents on the deal – or even losing money, if they have been trusting their automated software to set the price unattended. It's also possible that at some point one drop shipper had been intending to buy the book from someone further back on the chain. In any case, the book clearly ceases to exist at some point. Julius has to send an "out of stock" note to Fred, who then has to notify Bob, who tells you.

Even this level of chaos wouldn't be so bad, except that people who are out for a fast buck are notoriously lazy. In the previous example, things go reasonably well if everyone along the line is a diligent and scrupulous businessman, keeping close watch on their incoming orders. You could order in the morning, and find by evening that the purchase has failed, which is at least efficient. But let's say that each of them waits two days to check their in-box and place the order or respond. Allowing for weekends, you wouldn't find out for two weeks that your book wasn't in the mail. If you encounter someone who only places their orders every few days, when the mood strikes, the wait gets even longer. Since these sellers are probably inundated with queries from their buyers, they are motivated to set any e-mail aside that isn't making them more money.

To top it all off, a drop shipper doesn't have much of an idea of what is actually being sent out, and has to trust in the diligence and honesty of the actual holder of the item, however far down the line they happen to be. There is little room for accountability in these multiperson transactions. In the example, Bob could habitually ignore his orders for a week, even though Fred and Julius take action within two hours, and Julius could drastically underrate his books. The item would likely get to you within two weeks, and you would post enthusiastically positive feedback – for Bob, who is actually the laziest one of the bunch. On the other hand, if Bob and Fred are diligent, but Julius doesn't have any idea that he's doing someone else's business, and doesn't get around to pulling the item off his shelf for a few weeks – or sends an item that is substantially worse than described, or even the wrong item entirely – it is Bob who gets the worst possible rating from you.

Imagine that you are a college student. You need to take a certain class in order to graduate, but you weren't able to get a seat in the class until a week before the start of the semester, when someone else dropped it as an elective. By that time, all the textbooks are gone, though the college bookstore would happily order one, new, at a retail price of $156.95, and it would take four weeks to arrive. You go to Amazon, knowing that Marketplace merchants are *required* to ship in no more than two business days. You find the entry for the latest edition (with three new chapters vital to the class), and spot someone selling a Very Good copy for $99.99. You of course order it, gladly paying extra for Express shipping. Two weeks later, you've been able to photocopy some of the necessary pages from a friend's copy of the 700-page monster, but you're clearly beginning to lag behind in class, since you can neither follow along with the instructor or do any late-night studying. You start sending off queries to the seller but get no response. A month into the class, it finally arrives… and it's a beat-up, heavily marked photocopy of the previous edition, with "Not to be sold in the United

States" clearly printed on the cover. You might be able to recover your hundred bucks (plus shipping) in a month or two. Meantime, midterms are coming.

Sadly, that story is assembled from a handful of Feedback complaints I located in maybe two hours of searching. Since many of the merchants who cause this sort of disaster have dozens of Feedback entries per day, I likely missed a hundred older complaints – and those are only the buyers who took the time to write, meaning that there are probably as many again who have been burned in this manner. Please don't add to the woe.

To be fair, let's look at an actual example of how things *ought* to work out with listing services and multi-seller transactions. Recently, I bought a book through an EEB-type site based in Australia. The actual seller, though, has a bookstore in North Dakota. This worked out nicely for all three of us: the seller unloaded a low-demand book at a good price, I got exactly what I wanted without having to pay trans-oceanic shipping, and the broker got a percentage for bringing us together.

Watch your back

At the moment, Amazon.com tacitly encourages drop shipping, and even offers bits of advice to improve drop-shipping operations. However, if these abuses continue to escalate – and I am of the opinion that they are indeed escalating, both becoming more blatant and attracting wider abuse – then Amazon will have no choice but to crack down fiercely. When that happens, if you've put all your eggs in that basket, then you could find yourself summarily dumped from selling, even if you have been one of the most commendable examples. Drop ship if you must, but the Marketplace will be around in its present form for a lot longer – get up to speed, make sure that selling real items is your core business, and you will survive such sudden changes in policy.

In short, if you want to sell books and CDs, then sell books and CDs, don't just shuffle the listings around. If all you want to do is scrabble for a pile of cash, then at least have the decency to be utterly scrupulous about it.

Risks & thrills: book brokering

I don't recommend that you do what I'm about to describe, unless you either enjoy playing the stock market, or really know and love books. You could end up losing some money, or at least wasting plenty of time that could be spent more profitably.

Uncovering the phenomenon

I happened to have a certain mass paperback sitting on my personal shelves. I had bought it new in 1994 for $5.95, read it, enjoyed it greatly, then filed it. When we were getting up to speed on Amazon.com, I was looking up books as they occurred to me, and I wondered if this one had ever gone back into print. I was taken aback to find that it had never been reprinted, and that there were exactly five copies available, priced from $70 to $125.

I was stunned by both the demand and the lack of supply. Clearly, people want this title. I decided to make a few discreet queries to some real-world shops I deal with, figuring I could do worse than to buy a few copies at near SRP and selling them for maybe $25. Surprisingly, nobody had a copy available. Not one.

Dim memories from my days of studying the stock market surfaced. With this in mind, I had my item listed for $65, with a glowing description – I could testify that it was bought new, read once, and spotless but for a little shelfwear. It sold three weeks later.

Confirming my guess, a new listing of that title appeared two weeks after the sale, from the same small state as the person who'd bought mine, offering at $89.95.

The lurking danger

There's a phenomenon in investing known as the *bubble*.

Someone decides to invest heavily in something, possibly for reasons of sheer sentimentality or nostalgia. Someone else spots this, decides to buy in as well, sensing opportunity. This depletes what's available, so the "laws of supply and demand" kick in, and sellers raise their prices. More people buy, since now the price is beginning to climb and doesn't look like it'll stop soon. As the price inflates, more and more people jump on the bandwagon, driving the price up further.

Even if you haven't studied classic economic cases like the crazed market for Dutch tulips in the 17th century – so perfectly typical that the bubble phenomenon is sometimes called *tulipomania* – you can probably think of examples. The bubble in its purest form is just a bunch of get-rich-quick individuals; throw in a broker or a company who sees a way to make a buck from hyping the craziness, and the market doesn't inflate gracefully, but explodes into full blossom like a car's airbag during a collision.

Actually, that's a pretty good analogy, because as soon as a safety airbag hits full pressure… it deflates. That's why they call this market a *bubble* – it gets bigger and bigger until it can't grow any further, then it either explodes or collapses. You've seen this. Remember "Tickle-Me Elmo"? Furbies? The 1999 NASDAQ? Beanie Babies? Promises of a 15,000-point Dow Jones Industrial Average before 2001? Enron? Rookie cards? The "Magic: The Gathering" cardgame? In each case, a whole infrastructure springs up to take advantage of people who claim to be dyed-in-the-wool believers, but are really just hoping to make a fortune. Dedicated Internet sites proliferate, specialized magazines appear on the newsstands, grossly expensive "insider newsletters" stalk the land.

Then, one day, it all just dries up and blows away. A few years ago, every major chain store was selling packets of little cases you could put over the tags of your Beanie Babies to keep them intact and pristine; now you can't locate those cases without recourse to a few fanatic-run businesses, and the plush toys lie in heaps at thrift stores.

There are stories of companies who traded oil back and forth for years, not touching the commodity but exchanging paper representing loaded ships at berth; the value of this paper became increasingly valuable, right up until the moment someone decided to inspect the moored tankers, and they found not just empty holds, but no ships whatever. At least Elmo actually existed!

Avoid collapse

Brokering books doesn't *have* to be like that. In a pyramid game or Ponzi scheme, those people who get in early are the ones who make fortunes. (Or, rather, *could*: many times, they reinvest in the scheme, multiplying their profits again and again, right up until the scheme inevitably collapses.) The closer you are to the collapse when you sign up, the more you stand to lose. If you're dealing actual physical Amazon-listable items, you at least have an item with *some* intrinsic value. (If you unwittingly purchased a trashed item that shouldn't have been listed in the first place, you can exact some vengeance via the intercession of Amazon.com – and getting even has a *little* value.) By comparison, stock certificates for a collapsed company might number in the millions but they have no value, and aren't even good wallpaper.

With books, rising prices give an incentive for people to start looking around at bookstores, most of which price a used book and put it on the shelves where the price stays stable for years rather than following momentary changes in the market. A sharp bookseller, of course, keeps an eye on demand for rarer items and changes the price accordingly, not always upward; any fool can claim to have a shopful of $1,000 volumes, but this isn't very helpful when the landlord is expecting a rent payment, so prices need to drift downward to meet demand and the items get translated back into real dollars.

A bubble can make you a pleasant profit on Amazon.com, but when those other, cheaper volumes appear in the Marketplace, you don't want to find that you can't sell an item for as much as you paid in the first place. Here's an example: Recall that item I mentioned, that I sold at a tidy profit. I went back two months later, and found that there were more than a dozen now listed, about half of them priced at under $50 – supply had been dredged up to meet demand, and the prices were deflating. By accident, I had timed my sale well.

Weird pricing schemes

I'm satisfied that some of the people who list *really* high-priced books on Amazon.com are morons. Why would anyone of right mind even waste the time to list a common mass paperback for $1,220? Yes, we thought it was a typing error, but this seller has more than a dozen such titles. (Our staff expert on mystery novels has decided this merchant is selling drugs along with the books, which is far-fetched but would at least be a logical explanation.) Sure, a clueless customer might decide that the grossly overinflated pricetag denotes rarity, but you can't take this hope to the bank.

After seeing this phenomenon dozens of times, I made a joke that I was going to start listing all of our items for $666 each, with the description **Satan wants you to have this book**. After all, the profit margin is good. Then I decided that it would be a little creepy to be making contact with people who really *believe* that we are the retail outlet for the Prince of Darkness's personal book club. Maybe that's a niche that fits you better, and you're welcome to it.

You, too, can try out your pet theory. If you don't go wild on purchasing items for your inventory, the cost of experimenting is really nothing but your time.

Brokering tips

This is where the art of pricing really comes into its own. You might see ten copies of the only available edition selling for more than $12.95, and one lone listing for $1 that doesn't sound particularly worse than higher-priced copies,

You can gamble a little and buy the book, then see how you would rate it once it's actually in your hands. You might pay $4.49 with the shipping, then put it back out at $4.99, offering international shipping, and find a buyer who would be overjoyed to have it. Not a killing, but no loss except a little time – and you might instead find that the $1 book is actually like new, and worthy of being relisted at a high price.

Don't go overboard, though. Spending $75 with the intent to turn it around at $100 might find you waiting for your package as a dozen other sellers each list their own treasures at less than $20. Certainly, you might still locate a customer, but the chances go down that you will make any sort of profit in a reasonable amount of time.

Set yourself some standards, and stick to them rigidly. As a suggestion, don't buy an item for brokering unless you feel relatively certain that it will deserve to be listed for triple the total amount you pay. This will give you some flexibility if the one you receive isn't quite as solid an item as you'd believed. You likely won't have to take a loss even if you give up some of the profit you'd envisioned.

If the bubble deflates on you, then either take your loss and relist it at a lower price, or accept that it's going to be sitting on your shelf for a while. Don't overreact and slash your price on such an item: if the new supply meets only the first wave of demand, then you could sell your item within a year at a reasonable recovery.

Remember that the listings can skew your thinking. The reason so few copies of a title are listed may be because nobody wants it!

Forcing the price

I've heard about a grand scheme to artificially control the "market" on Amazon.com. I'm going to briefly explain it because I don't want to think you're dumb enough to try it yourself. And I don't want you to try it because you're likely to get badly burned, as well as messing up some of the fun part of trading for buyers and sellers like me.

The seller decided that, since a certain title was selling fairly well at $15 and up, but the Marketplace also had a few dozen one-cent copies available, he would buy up all of the low-end books and relist them for $15 or more. As the demand increased, he would simply pull his own low-end listings and raise them another dollar or two. Customers who were waiting to buy would take note of this, and leap to buy before the prices swelled again.

There are many reasons this failed. Very few customers are hovering in indecision: items on Amazon.com are largely impulse buys, but that impulse is often shaped by very specific interests. Poking at these people with the pointy stick of threatened price increase is more likely to drive them away than to make them buy. On the supply side, kicking the prices up only gives other entrepreneurs a monetary incentive to undercut the gougers.

You might be able to turn a profit on this bubble, buying from one would-be broker and selling to another, but you could also find yourself stuck with a book nobody wants when the music stops.

These two methods of jacking up the price are nothing new, and simply reflect two forces that have affected the rare-book market for centuries. Both brokering and forcing depend not just upon the market scarcity of an item, but upon demand. Forcing is partially predicated upon the idea that someone is going to buy that item simply because it's scarce – in other words, a bubble. Brokering can take advantage of this, of course, but depends more heavily upon an honest demand for the book by individuals who want to read a scarce title, and a smaller group who fancy themselves collectors.

Brokering and forcing are both tricks to artificially manipulate price and availability, and they both present significant risks to players. The difference, though, is that brokering is a way of working with existing market forces, and in the long run encourages people to hunt down hard-to-find items and add them to the listings. Forcing is built upon a combination of greed and stupidity, working from the reverse assumption that a market can be cornered, and then kept cornered while it is bled for profit. Most people who try to corner a market will, sooner or later, be tripped up by their own arrogance; they'll take "just one more" dip into the buy-sell cycle, expend all their capital (and maybe some credit as well on this "sure thing"), then find themselves far up in the sky when their imaginary mountain suddenly disappears.

An example of brokering

Brokering is not merely fun, but gives me the not-so-guilty pleasure of taking advantage of people who are trying to force the market. Recall my example of the $5.95 book we sold for $65. That particular bubble fluctuates but it's still alive on Amazon, because the item is honestly scarce. Our little company has friends all over the publishing trade. What would happen if one of these friends found a dusty unopened case of that title, and was overjoyed to sell it to us for retail price?

Here's how we'd handle that situation. Given the prices on

the Marketplace as I write, I'd select the worst in the caseload, and put it out for $30 as "Used – Good." I'd take about the fifth-best, and list it as "Collectible – New," for at least $50. They would both probably be snapped up within a week, and relisted two weeks later at almost double. The buyers would do that because they're seeing this as a closed system, whereas I'm working from knowledge that the system is open – I've got an inventory, a stock, not just a single item. They not only don't know how many aces I have in my hand, they don't know how many cards I'm holding. By not listing more than one or two, I maintain the illusion of scarcity, lending a little justification to the price I set.

As soon as I sold one, I'd list another in similar or better shape, at a slightly higher price. It's not a stretch for me to guess that there are one or two typical customers who were considering that item, and were a little disappointed when it was sold. When I set out another to fill the empty space on the virtual shelf, a dithering buyer will sometimes jump at the next offering, especially if it sounds to be at least as good as the one that got away.

Of course, this is about the point where some smart-aleck sees what's going on, raids every Goodwill store in a fifty-mile radius, and finds four copies, which show up on the Marketplace at $20 each. I don't see this as "competition," and certainly not a bad thing. In fact, I enjoy this because it brings more players into the game, encourages entrepreneurship, and adds choice to the Amazon.com jungle. If there is truly a demand to justify high prices, then those lower-priced items will be gone soon enough, and I'm back in the game.

(Furthermore, I have sometimes written an e-mail to a new player, saying, "Welcome! But a bit of friendly advice – DOUBLE YOUR PRICE. You've got a scarce item!" We saved one guy from selling a numbered limited-edition set for retail prices, though we could've made a nice profit by reselling it ourselves. On the other hand, he's now encouraged to stay with the game, to keep looking for thrift-store bargains and bringing them to the Marketplace, where book nuts like me are always on the hunt for some terribly obscure title.)

(For what it's worth: communication between Amazon merchants is expressly forbidden – technically, at least. This is because of legalistic fear that merchants will collude in some sort of price fixing scheme. Actually, we chatter quite a bit in the Amazon-sponsored Discussion Boards, and – as detailed in this chapter and the previous – there is already a surplus of overt scams taking place. Nevertheless, it's good etiquette to not harass other people via e-mail, so don't get too casual about it.)

By this point in the brokering game, if there are forcers buying up my items and relisting them at even more inflated prices, they're overextended. If I'm feeling mean, and I've still got a few copies of that title, I might list them all at once, at perhaps half what I'm asking for the others. This gives regular customers a chance to snap up a bargain (and I'm still making a nice profit), but the forcers would be in the awkward position of buying even more of the very item they can't sell.

If we play the game long enough, the out-of-print book might come out in a new edition. At that point, I'm still ahead of the game, since I can probably sell an earlier edition for up to 50% more than the new book's SRP. The forcers, though, are in over their heads, and would probably be better off selling out their stock of that title at a loss.

Other sales sites

This is not a comprehensive list, but will be enough so that you can look around. Keep an eye on the Amazon seller forums, as merchants frequently mention alternatives for items that don't fit well into their Amazon presence. For the most part you're on your own as to whether you sell at one of these sites, buy from them, or just read their FAQs for marketing ideas – what, I'm supposed to give away *all* our trade secrets? All I can tell you is that, last I checked, all of the links below worked sometime in 2004.

Well, okay, a few hints. I chose these from a list of companies I occasionally purchase from. There are books, of course, as well as CDs, and if you're going to make a steady trade of CDs then you'll need a source for good inexpensive cases. I've also tossed in a few for wholesale jewelry, discount stereo stuff, and office supplies, in case your zShop looks a little bare. The URLs at the end are a few suggestions of interesting stuff that could be sold on a zShop (or the equivalent elsewhere, like eBay). Above all, don't forget to check out the Amazon sites in other countries – as I write these words, the Marketplace is up and running in Canada and the United Kingdom, and it's also begun in France and Germany, though my Japanese isn't good enough that I can check that site. (No, you can't *sell* on those sites, unless you happen to have the inventory and a bank account in that country.)

www.onlinebookselling.net – This site was apparently created by Stephen Windwalker to support his books, *Selling Used Books Online* and *Buying Books Online*. Though I can't find that any transactions are actually taking place here, and the information appears to be woefully out of date (the home page says it was last updated April 15, 2003), it's an admirably massive compendium of links about bookselling. Give it some serious scrutiny, and maybe toss a few dollars to the owners via PayPal if they steer you toward a few gems of advice.

www.half.com – Supposed to be closed in 2004, since it was purchased a few years ago by eBay, which has incorporated most of its niche into their main site. Still, it might be around when this book comes out, and it never hurts to check all available outlets whether you're scrounging for bargains or for that one specific item.

www.eBay.com – Don't overlook scrolling all the way down the left-side list of the home page; at the bottom is one marked **Wholesale** that will take you right to a special page for wholesale lots of various kinds of stuff. Ditto for *www.eBay.co.uk* and *www.eBay.co.au* and *www.eBay.co.ca* so that you can keep up with the possibilities in the English-speaking world – if you have some skill with other languages, you could find yourself purchasing from up to a dozen other nations that eBay specifically intends to serve. For the most part, everything appears to show up on the main eBay site.

www.GEMM.com – My company has only recently started with GEMM, which specializes in music of all sorts. If you're going to present a stock of LPs and 8-track tapes, you might find this site handier than a zShop. Imagine a Marketplace with no centralized database, and very few bells or whistles. Unlike Amazon, GEMM offers a wider choice of payment and shipping options, and otherwise much of the same functionality you would expect from a zShop. You are expected to type in the name of the artist and the title of the item, which can result in great confusion, especially among the spelling-impaired.

www.GEMMbooks.com

www.bookbyte.com

auctions.shopping.yahoo.com

www.bn.com

www.pricetag.com

Other sales sites

www.alibris.com
www.bookfinder.com
www.biblio.com
www.booksamillion.com
www.booksareeverything.com
www.booksellersnow.com
www.choosebooks.com
www.zooba.com
www.musicstack.com
www.esotericism.co.uk
store.DoverPublications.com
www.newleafvendors.com
www.used-books-search.com
www.powells.com
www.halfvalue.com
www.overstock.com
www.savers.com
www.NexTag.com
www.TtaDirect.com
www.buy.com
www.Overstock.com
www.bid4assets.com
www.BizRate.com
www.FrederickBuechner.net
www.ePier.com
www.CDRack.com
www.cdconnection.com
musicwormer.com
www.WholesalersCatalog.com
www.WholesaleMusicCds.com
www.MoonlightSales.com
www.Wholesale411.com

www.4DealersOnly.com
www.CDPriceFind.com
www.wholesaledistributorsnet.com
www.CDDVDLiquidation.com
www.CoffeeHouseMusic.com
www.WholesaleRAMP.com
www.booksalefinder.com
www.independentbands.com
www.wholesalediscs.com
www.surplusrecords.com
www.tothetrade.co.uk
www.CyberMusicSurplus.com
www.way2bid.com
www.oneway.co.nz
www.eWanted.com

Other stuff you could sell

www.gemhut.com
www.firemountaingems.com
www.merlite.com
www.CafeShops.com
www.GetEstore.com

The last words

So, c'mon – jump in!

It doesn't cost much, or demand a significant time commitment. If you love books, it's a cheap education. You won't get rich, but you almost have to go out of your way to *not* make a profit. With the stuff you've read in this little book, you're already ahead of the game.

We'll see you there!

Index